The
Colour Scheme
Sourcebook

The
Colour Scheme
Sourcebook

Learn how to combine colours
to achieve the look you desire

ANNA STARMER

APPLE

APPLE

A QUARTO BOOK

QUAR.CSBB

Published by Apple Press
7 Greenland Street
London NW1 0ND
www.apple-press.com

Copyright © 2005 Quarto Publishing plc
Reprinted 2007

10 9 8 7 6 5 4 3 2

ISBN 978 1 84543 044 3

This book was designed and produced by
Quarto Publishing plc
The Old Brewery
6 Blundell Street
London N7 9BH

Art Editor Anna Knight, Stephen Minns
Designer Louise Clements, Karin Skanberg
Project Editor Trisha Telep
Picture Researcher Claudia Tate
Assistant Art Director Penny Cobb

Art Director Moira Clinch
Publisher Piers Spence

Manufactured in Singapore by Chroma Graphics
Printed in Hong Kong by Midas Printing Ltd.

Contents

How to use *this book*

This book contains 200 inspirational colour palettes for home decorators and interior designers. The text accompanying each palette discusses the moods the colours evoke, and will help you create your desired ambience. There is also practical application guidance, which will help you approach the room as a whole, and advice on the kind of finishing touches that suit the particular scheme.

At the beginning of the book you will find information on colour theory, along with some ideas on how to create your own schemes and designs. While it is helpful to have some basic understanding of colour theory and principles, it is also important to create a room that you, your family and your friends are going to enjoy. You can also use the world around you as a source of inspiration, gathering tips and ideas from everyday life, and learning to really enjoy colour.

To help you make your own colour choices at home, the book is separated into nine colour chapters: Pinks, Reds, Oranges and Browns, Yellows, Greens, Blues, Violets, Neutrals and Greys. Each chapter contains many levels and tones of colour, from bright, pure primaries through to delicate, tinted pales. We have chosen some classic colour combinations with an almost timeless quality, as well as contemporary schemes that can bring a fresh look to any style of house.

Using the palettes

(1) Colour-coded bullets correspond to the colour chapter that you're in.

(2) Mood-enhancing words to help you imagine the feeling each scheme will evoke.

(3) The inspiration behind the colour choices. This section tells you about the main colour for the room.

(4) This is the theory behind the interior-design style. Find ideas and inspiration on materials and finishes, flooring, furniture, pattern and accessories.

(5) The main colour in the room, to be used on all, or most of, the wall space. Take this book to your local DIY shop and ask them to match a

test pot to this colour. Paint a square of colour on your chosen wall and let it dry, as paint always changes colour when it dries. Live with the colour for a day or two to see if you really do love it before committing to a whole room.

(6) Alongside the main hue are slightly differing tones of the same

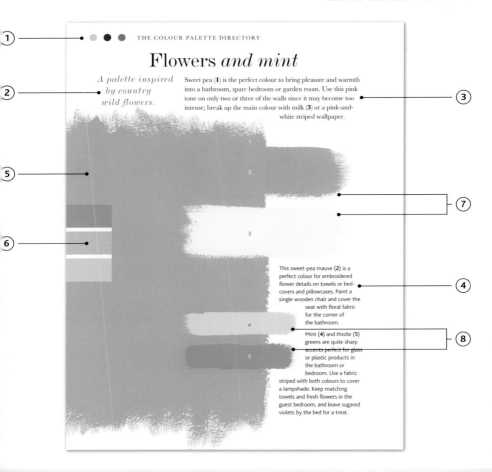

THE COLOUR PALETTE DIRECTORY

Flowers *and mint*

A palette inspired by country wild flowers.

Sweet pea (**1**) is the perfect colour to bring pleasure and warmth into a bathroom, spare bedroom or garden room. Use this pink tone on only two or three of the walls since it may become too intense; break up the main colour with milk (**3**) or a pink-and-white striped wallpaper.

This sweet-pea mauve (**2**) is a perfect colour for embroidered flower details on towels or bed-covers and pillowcases. Paint a single wooden chair and cover the seat with floral fabric for the corner of the bathroom.

Mint (**4**) and thistle (**5**) greens are quite sharp accents perfect for glass or plastic products in the bathroom or bedroom. Use a fabric striped with both colours to cover a lampshade. Keep matching towels and fresh flowers in the guest bedroom, and leave sugared violets by the bed for a treat.

colour. If you are not entirely happy with the main colour, this is the place to look for an alternative.

(**7**) The accent colours can be used for an adjacent wall, for woodwork or to match to upholstery fabrics. The colours may be darker or lighter tones of the main shade, neutral shades to balance a room or complementary colours that create a contrast in an interior.

(**8**) Each scheme also features two highlight colours. These can take the form of a sharp injection of colour against a pale wall, such as a red glass vase in a pale blue interior; or the final balancing tone in a range of harmonious colours, such as deep chocolate brown in a room of luxurious coffee tones. The highlight colours, although only used in small quantities, are often the most important shades of all since they complete the design.

Colour in the home

A house is much more than just a roof over our heads. Our places of dwelling have developed dramatically over the course of history. Homes today have to be incredibly versatile buildings, often serving as a restaurant, nursery, hotel, office, library and sanctuary. The places in which we live should be enjoyed, provide protection, respite, peace, inspiration and warmth to all who enter.

Mix modern with traditional: use contrasting elements such as pale aqua with a highlight of bold neon orange, or ornate French furniture with soft metallics and bright, shiny acrylic plastic.

Colour can dramatically alter any space within a home. The possibilities made available to us by modern paints are almost limitless, and traditional and modern homes alike can be transformed through the clever use of colour. Pale colours and whites can instantly refresh a tired room, giving a clean look and creating a bright, spacious atmosphere. Rich colours, such as deep ruby or emerald green, will have an intense effect, creating a more intimate and cosy feeling.

Colour in the home cannot be changed as often as we change our clothing, so the colour decision is extremely important. This book aims to help you choose that all-important scheme, and to ensure that the choice suits your lifestyle and meets your personal and emotional needs.

Colour for today

Colour is one of the most exciting raw materials on earth. Since the beginning of time people have been using colour to mark territory and decorate their surroundings. Colour is powerful – it can cleanse and revive a tired area in any home, and can change a mood and lift the spirits. Across the globe different cultures attach significance to certain colours. Colour can be passionate and sensual, and it can be calming and meditative.

Colours make an impression on all of us, and colour and texture help to make our world a fascinating and beautiful place to live. Yet colour is a reasonably modern luxury. Only 100 years ago colour was the preserve of the wealthy, and there was no colour television, no glossy colour magazines or books, no plastics and limited textile dyes. For the majority, the world was simply many shades of grey.

However, in the 1950s the chemical industry made it possible to produce many more colours in dye and paint. It is possible today to create over 16 million separate colours. Developments in paint technology have also meant that we can now buy thousands of different paint types, ranging from basic emulsions through to metallic finishes, eco-friendly natural paints, and even magnetic paint.

Colour with confidence

Using paint is a simple and cost-effective way to completely restore and revive any area in the home. Never before has there been such a wide choice of colour in paints, wallpapers, furniture and fabrics, allowing us to make our own designs and statements with colour. But with so much choice, where do we begin? With all these possibilities, making colour choices for the home can confuse and intimidate both the amateur and professional decorator. Many paint manufacturers boast that they can match almost any colour, which is an incredible resource. But how can we decide on that perfect shade?

Enliven a tired guest room. Lavender is warmed up with fiery orange and bright magenta highlights. A bold use of pattern is a truly confident way to finish this welcoming guest interior.

This book can help you choose the right colour for you, your room and its situation, and then show you how to build a stunning interior design around that colour. Choosing the correct scheme for a room can transform a space from a tired living area into a stylish one. The right decisions made early on can have dramatic effects, which will not only impress your friends and family, but could even add value to your property. This book will arm you with the theoretical knowledge, a little inspiration, and a conviction in your own tastes that in turn will give you the confidence you need to use colour to its full potential.

SPEAKING PRACTICALLY

There are many factors to consider before you begin the work of filling a space with colour. A small amount of practical knowledge and creative inspiration can go a long way in helping you to make the right choices. When choosing colours for your home, ask yourself some of these questions:

- What is the room to be used for?
- Who uses the room the most?
- What time of day will the room be used the most?
- How much natural light does the room receive?
- What important architectural features are there in the room?
- Which large pieces of furniture are, or will be, in the room?
- Which colours are featured in the rooms directly adjacent to the room?
- What feelings and emotions do you want the room to convey?

Write down your answers to these questions and keep them in mind as you peruse the information and visual references in this book. You will soon hit upon the perfect colour scheme for your room.

Deciphering the Rainbow

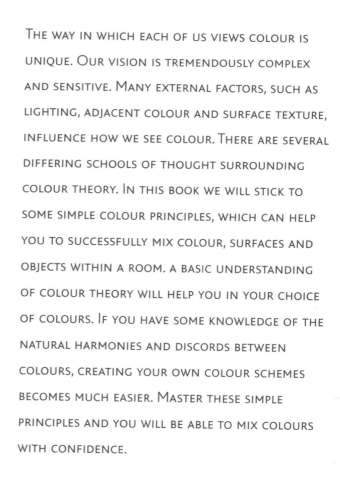

THE WAY IN WHICH EACH OF US VIEWS COLOUR IS UNIQUE. OUR VISION IS TREMENDOUSLY COMPLEX AND SENSITIVE. MANY EXTERNAL FACTORS, SUCH AS LIGHTING, ADJACENT COLOUR AND SURFACE TEXTURE, INFLUENCE HOW WE SEE COLOUR. THERE ARE SEVERAL DIFFERING SCHOOLS OF THOUGHT SURROUNDING COLOUR THEORY. IN THIS BOOK WE WILL STICK TO SOME SIMPLE COLOUR PRINCIPLES, WHICH CAN HELP YOU TO SUCCESSFULLY MIX COLOUR, SURFACES AND OBJECTS WITHIN A ROOM. A BASIC UNDERSTANDING OF COLOUR THEORY WILL HELP YOU IN YOUR CHOICE OF COLOURS. IF YOU HAVE SOME KNOWLEDGE OF THE NATURAL HARMONIES AND DISCORDS BETWEEN COLOURS, CREATING YOUR OWN COLOUR SCHEMES BECOMES MUCH EASIER. MASTER THESE SIMPLE PRINCIPLES AND YOU WILL BE ABLE TO MIX COLOURS WITH CONFIDENCE.

A harmonious palette of oranges and golds. A soft pumpkin wall colour is enhanced by complementary accents from one colour family.

Colour *theory*

Colour is taken for granted today as an intrinsic part of every waking moment. It is beneficial, however, to make a point of learning how the human eye perceives colour. The following scientific principles can be used as much or as little as you like. They can help you to make decorating decisions that will turn a simple colour scheme into a successful interior.

Isaac Newton (1642–1727) explained that colour originates in light. After much experimentation he worked out that light is made up of several different colours, and when he refracted light through a prism he was presented with the seven colours of the rainbow: red, orange, yellow, green, cyan (light blue), indigo (dark blue) and violet. Newtonian principles are still used today.

Thomas Young (1773–1829) took Newton's studies one step further when he realised that just three of the colours in the rainbow make up white light: red, green and blue. These three colours are the original primary colours. In 1859 the German physiologist Herman Von Helmholtz (1821–1894) built on Young's work and developed the theory that our eyes read colour in terms of light, in red, green and blue. This theory was widely accepted and showed that every object is 'coded' or broken down by the brain into various percentages of red, green and blue, which is how we see colour.

Hering's colour wheel

On this wheel, yellow is the fourth 'primary' colour. Ewald Hering (1834-1918) opposed the teachings of Helmholtz, believing that his chart gave a truer indication of the human experience of colour. He argued that yellow ought to be a primary colour because it is seen by the eye as an independent colour, along

All surfaces absorb and reflect light, breaking it down into separate colours. The human eye can only see the colours that are reflected. This is how we visualise colour.

Green   Black   White

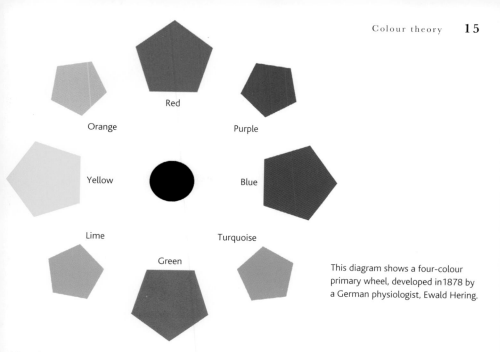

Red

Orange Purple

Yellow Blue

Lime Turquoise

Green

This diagram shows a four-colour primary wheel, developed in 1878 by a German physiologist, Ewald Hering.

with red, green and blue. He also included black and white as basic visual primary colours. Hering described his order of colours as 'the natural system of colour sensations'. Today his system forms the basis of the NCS, the Natural Colour System, which is used all over the world as a colour-matching tool.

HARMONIOUS COLOURS

The four 'primary' colours are red, blue, green and yellow. When these pure colours are mixed, the secondary colours of purple, turquoise, orange and lime are produced. As you move around the wheel you can immediately see the harmonies between the colours that are adjacent to each other. For instance, a palette made up of tones of yellow, lemon, marigold and terracotta will always be successful. These colours all originate from between yellow and orange on the colour wheel and they have an intrinsic harmony with each other.

COMPLEMENTARY COLOURS

Colours that sit opposite each other on the colour wheel are called 'complementary'. These are opposing colours that vibrate against each other, or clash. Often you will not see complementary colours together in a scheme, but sometimes the clever use of a complementary colour in a room can have a striking effect. For instance, a bright turquoise chair against a soft orange-peach wall would look wonderful.

Colours to suit *you*

A little knowledge can go a long way, but rules are made to be broken. We can all be influenced by scientific theory and the current trends, but just remember the most important thing: it is you and your family who have to live with and enjoy these colours.

Use colours and pattern to really suit you, even if they are a little unusual or eccentric.

Never forget your own personal preferences and inspirations. If you simply love rich, jewel-like shades, then be bold and go for a luscious raspberry to inspire you in your work area. You can use your knowledge of the colour wheel to perfect the actual shades and intensity of the colours, but do not be afraid to go with exactly what you love.

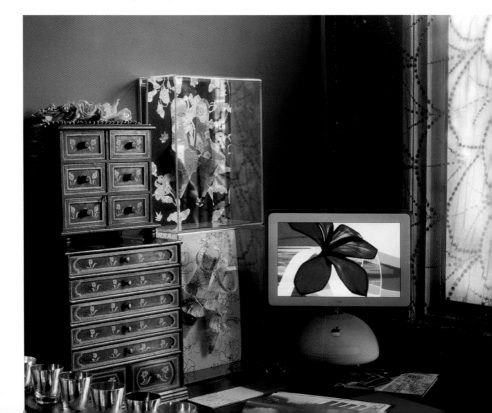

Simple colour rules

Colour began to be more widely available in home interiors after World War II. Particularly in Europe, after years of rationing during the war, colour in the home seemed like a real luxury. During this period, a set of rules evolved, stating which colours worked best together. These are a good basis upon which to build ideas, but with so many more paint colours, application techniques and surfaces available to us today, we can easily go beyond these basic principles.

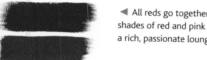

◀ All reds go together, as do all pinks. Certain shades of red and pink together can be great for a rich, passionate lounge or a pastel, floral bedroom.

▶ Soft oranges are fantastically warming, and darker oranges must be used in moderation.

◀ Browns look great with orange. Turquoise and cool greys are good complementary colours to orange.

▶ Yellows go well with greens and oranges. Blues and yellows (complementary colours) create a classic interior combination for an upbeat, fresh environment.

◀ Green is often used like a neutral colour to balance a room since certain shades of green, such as soft sage, can go with almost any other colour.

▶ All blues go together, and all greens go together. Shades of blue and green are fantastic together at all levels of intensity, from pale sky and duck egg through to dark inks and peacocks.

◀ Shades of violet can work well together, but may be too overpowering for most. Violets also look great with greens. Blue violets work well with cool blues, and red violets look beautiful with soft pinks.

▶ Greys and neutrals mix together well for a classic backdrop of unobtrusive tones, and such 'colourless' palettes have been popular in the past and continue to be used today. Almost any colour can be mixed with neutrals and greys to create unusual and stunning interiors.

Colour and Mood

Every room in a house has the ability to evoke a mood and an atmosphere. A soft green bathroom can be a relaxing, calming environment, while a bright yellow entrance hall is warming and uplifting. Colour, light and texture can stimulate the senses and awaken our emotions. our homes can become a haven of mood-enhancing spaces to calm the soul and refresh the mind.

One of the most important aspects of decorating is creating the right kind of mood for you, an environment where you can be relaxed, comfortable, happy and content. If you are clever with paint, fabrics and lighting, you can dramatically alter the mood of a room and create a space tailor-made to your own lifestyle and emotional needs.

An elegant use of soft greens.
Simple, yet pretty accents in pinks
and pale blues help to create a
calming, meditative mood.

Looking at *light*

Most of us do not usually consider the effects of light when decorating our home. Yet light can be the single most important element in making a scheme work. Living so much of our lives in artificial light, we often forget about the effects of changing light throughout the day, and how the passing of the seasons affects the way we see colour.

Light coming in

Natural light keeps the world alive and you should take full advantage of it. Try to maximize the amount of daylight in your home with as many windows and skylights as possible. Make the most of strong summer sunlight by using the lightest, most diaphanous curtains at the windows in a bedroom or kitchen, which will let the wonderful light flood in. If an entrance seems very dark, consider a frosted glass door, which will let a diffused light through. Alternatively, use a block of bold colour, such as geranium pink, on a single wall to lift the atmosphere of the area. It is often difficult to change the architectural details of a room, but clever use of colour and light can easily make the most of any dark area in your home.

Make the most of natural light with large windows, glass panelled doors and pale colours on all the walls.

When deciding on a colour scheme for a particular room, you need to consider the natural light that enters into it. Find out how strong the daylight is and spend some time in the room at different times of day, taking note of how the light affects it. For instance, if a room is facing north-east in the northern hemisphere, it will receive the least amount of natural light, so always use warming colours in this room to soften the shadows. If a bathroom has a large window and receives lots of natural light for most of the day, then a palette of cool blues and violets would look pretty, not cold.

Remember that at different times of the year, a room can take on different personalities. Just as the garden dies off in the autumn, so the house becomes darker, curtains are closed earlier and more artificial lighting is used. You may wish to choose a scheme that works as well in daylight as in artificial light, such as warm mauves or coffee colours. Create a more cosy look in the dark winter months by simply changing bedspreads and cushions from crisp cotton to brushed flannels, velvets or fake fur. Place rugs or sheepskins on any bare flooring and drape soft, richly coloured blankets on the backs of chairs and sofas.

Create a cosy atmosphere in a dark area with the use of soft lighting, and warming colours like reds and oranges.

Mood-creating light

Artificial light is a necessary part of our lives. Today there are many types of lighting available and it is a good idea to consider alternatives to overhead lighting, since it can be unflattering and harsh. Think about the activity that will take place in the room, and direct the light accordingly.

There are three main areas of lighting to consider. The first is task lighting, good, strong light used for working, cooking or reading. To achieve this, use daylight bulbs for a clearer view, and adjustable or telescopic lamps to direct the light. The second is ambient lighting, which is the general lighting in a room. It is often too bright, so choose low-level lighting or wall lights for a softer feel, and install a dimmer switch. Lastly, mood lighting is used to create a certain atmosphere, often a soft, romantic or intimate light. It should be kept at a low level – candles are perfect for creating a cosy, gentle mood.

Task lighting (below): Directional lighting aids specific needs such as reading or preparing food.

Mood lighting (right): Low-level, atmospheric lighting is perfect for quiet evenings at home.

Colour and *emotions*

We are all emotional creatures and the modern world constantly inspires emotions within us. Being in a forest can make you feel peaceful, while sitting in a bright yellow café can make you feel stimulated or happy. However, often we are not aware of the effects the visual world has on our senses and our feelings.

A bold use of blues is exciting and inspiring. A surprise accent colour lifts the spirit of any interior.

Certain colours can evoke a strong emotional response, and clever use of light can enhance or subdue a mood. So before you decorate, take the time to first consider how you want to feel in the room, and spend some time there before you decide on the final palette. Paint some test colours on the walls and observe how they change from day to night, and drape some fabric over a chair in front of the painted wall to see how the two colours and surfaces react with each other.

For example, in a home office that benefits from lots of natural daylight, you may wish to use a cool sky blue as the main colour in order to stimulate clear thinking and a peaceful atmosphere. Yellow is a great colour to use in a kitchen, and creates a citrus-fresh wake-up or, if a warmer tone is used, a cosy family space. If you decide on a passionate, hot-blooded scheme of red tones for the living room, then consider surfaces and fabrics that will enhance this sensual mood. Choose a high-gloss lipstick colour for the woodwork and sumptuous velvets and smooth satins for the upholstery. Low-level candlelight is sure to finish this mood off perfectly.

Mood enhancers

There are several emotions that certain colour groups have been recognised as inspiring. These emotions can be altered dramatically depending on the depth or tone of the colour, but the basic principles are worth remembering when deciding on your colour palette.

Pinks are fun, lively, positive and feminine.

Reds are passionate, daring, intimate and comforting.

Oranges stimulate creativity and are warming and cosy.

Yellows are welcoming and sunny. Strong yellows are said
to help the brain work better.

Greens represent nature and are both tranquil and invigorating, as well
as restful and balancing.

Blues are connected to the sky and to water, and they are associated
with clear thinking and calm, meditative environments.

Violets can be stimulating and sexy, while blue violets can be cooling and spiritual.

Finding Inspiration

Whether you live in a city or in the country, there is plenty to inspire. Simply take a little extra time to stop and look around. Consider the colour combinations used by advertisers on posters or food packaging. These colours have been carefully matched by graphic designers, so it is no accident that they look good together. Remember the colours on the walls of your favourite restaurant. Collect fallen leaves to inspire a palette of rich oranges and ochres. Look closely at the many tones in a menacing grey, stormy sky against the warm brown bark of a tree. Visit an art gallery and look closely at the tones and shades used by classical and contemporary artists. You can find inspiration anywhere if you take a few moments to seek it out.

Take inspiration from the world around you. These weathered boats could be translated into a fantastic kitchen filled with green-and-blue-painted wooden cupboards.

Using *colour scrapbooks*

Start carrying a small notebook around with you, and even a mini camera to keep track of your colour observations. Collect bus tickets, sweet wrappers, magazine pages, restaurant cards and flyers, and stick them in your book.

A rich, vibrant colour scrapbook featuring your favourite items is the perfect base on which to build a great colour library.

Take note of how colours you see make you feel, like how a field of bright red poppies can put a smile on your face, or how a woman's purple scarf against a grey sky can make you feel melancholy. Collecting colours is a fantastic game – suddenly your world becomes a huge painter's palette of inspiration and choice, and even the daily commute to work can become fun and interesting.

How to make a *mood board*

Mood boards are creative tools used by most designers, from fashion to interiors. A mood board is a visual story that is used to inspire a design team, or to explain to a client a certain design concept.

An inspirational collection of items to help in choosing specific colours, patterns and combinations.

Mood boards can be created from almost anything. They should be a considered representation of your research and taste. Look at the objects, photographs, cuttings, paint chips, fabrics and wallpaper swatches that you have collected. A favourite colour scheme and style will begin to emerge. Once the mood board is finalised, use it as a constant reference throughout the decorating process.

Method

On a large board, lay out the reference materials you have gathered and consider how they look together. Play with scale, proportion and colour on the board and try to find a harmonious combination. To do this, you can enlarge or reduce the size of specific items by using a colour photocopier. Consider the colours that will be used most prominently in the room, for walls and floors for example, and try to display smaller pieces against these backdrop colours. Now try to visualise the proportion of colour and pattern in your chosen room. This may take some imagination, so take the mood board into the room to help. Professional interior designers will often include a sketch of the intended final layout on a mood board to help the client visualise the end result. Try it for yourself.

A professional mood board of glossy images, colours, textures and fabrics was created as inspiration for the interior on the facing page.

The finished interior

A beautifully harmonious, yet modern bedroom interior was created from the information gathered in the mood board.

It is worth taking the time to learn a little about colour, light and texture, and to learn which colours you personally love, before you start to decorate any area in the home. The mood board should be a considered conclusion to all of your research, and the final room will be a perfect interpretation of the mood that you have envisioned. The softened mauve of this room is dusted and flat, creating a perfect backdrop upon which to use rich colour and bold textures. So mauve looks delicious with deep chocolates, a bold highlight is needed to lift the colours and add a modern edge. The geranium-pink silk cushion adds a touch of glamour to the dark, quilted bed covers, the pink pattern contrasts well with the understated texture of the chocolate velvet bedspread. The bright magenta vase and pink flowers pick up on the highlight colour once again in polished glass, which catches the light perfectly. Different surfaces play with the diffused light in the room from hard mirror and glass to soft velvets and silks.

The Colour Palette Directory

THIS EASY-TO-USE CHART ILLUSTRATES THE MAIN COLOURS IN THE 200 PALETTES. AT A GLANCE YOU CAN SELECT A COLOUR, THEN TURN TO THE CORRECT PAGE AND DISCOVER HOW TO USE IT EFFECTIVELY IN A PARTICULAR ROOM SCHEME.

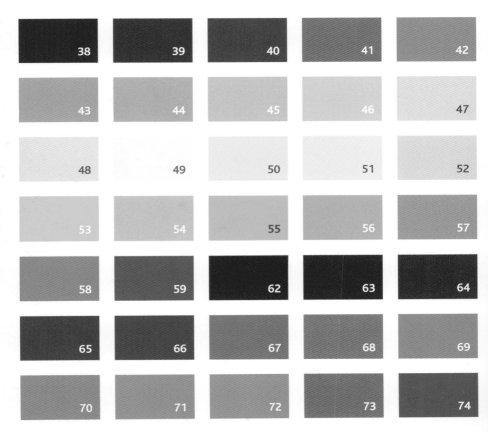

75	76	77	78	79
82	83	84	85	86
87	88	89	90	91
92	93	94	95	96
97	98	99	100	101
102	103	104	105	108
109	110	111	112	113
114	115	116	117	118
119	120	121	122	123
124	125	126	127	128
129	130	131	134	135

136	137	138	139	140
141	142	143	144	145
146	147	148	149	150
151	152	153	154	155
156	157	160	161	162
163	164	165	166	167
168	169	170	171	172
173	174	175	176	177
178	179	180	181	182
183	184	185	186	187
190	191	192	193	194

195	196	197	198	199
200	201	202	203	204
205	206	207	208	209
210	211	212	213	216
217	218	219	220	221
222	223	224	225	226
227	228	229	230	231
232	233	236	237	238
239	240	241	242	243
244	245	246	247	248
249	250	251	252	253

Pinks

Intense, *elegant and refined*

A striking play of dark and light needs precise design.

Cranberry (**1**) is contrasted with softened tones, a clever juxtaposition of colours that needs a precise, geometric plan to be successful. Dark colours draw in the room and need areas of light in order to prevent the atmosphere from becoming too sombre. This truly modern palette evokes quality and good taste.

Tradition is knocked on the head here as darker tones are used for the walls and soft, delicate shades for the woodwork. Dusky pink (**2**) and soft stone (**3**) are classic interior colours and they add a touch of sensitivity to this strong, modern palette.

Sage green (**4**) balances the room with cool undertones, preventing the pinks from getting too pretty.

Black (**5**) has once again become very chic in interior design. Use on very glossy surfaces such as glass or lacquer. Try black serving plates in the dining room – they really complement the colours of food.

Raspberry *crushed velvet*

Rich and luscious raspberry (**1**) gives an instant feeling of
sumptuousness. The highlight colours in this room are traditional
interior colours from the turn of the last century. By combining
such softened mid-tones with hot pink a truly contemporary
interpretation is reached.

*Soft, cosy vintage
tones are fused
with modern berry.*

Warm and inviting, flat paints
complement these dusty colours.
Other surfaces in this room should
be textural and tactile, like suede,
knitted mohair or velvet.

Sueded buff (**2**) can be
used for the flooring
and larger pieces of
furniture in the room,
while mid-pink (**3**) is a
perfect complement to
the raspberry walls.

Accessorize in soft
lavender (**4**) and smooth
chocolate (**5**) for that added edge
of grown-up sophistication.

This palette is perfect for a dining
room or living area, where you will
feel cosy, confident and creative.

Nostalgia *and naive memories*

Retro colours from the 1950s inspire a simple, easy palette.

This wonderfully intense magenta (**1**) is brought down to earth with a trip down memory lane. Look to old-fashioned children's storybook illustrations for colour inspiration. A typically 1950s approach to using colour can once again look new in this simple yet stylish design.

Use the darker cobalt (**3**) as the woodwork colour and baby blue (**2**) for textiles. For curtains and cushions, mix the blues in stripes reminiscent of ship's deck chairs.

Poppy (**4**) and snapdragon (**5**) can be used as accessory colours within the room for a real nostalgic touch. These pleasing sunset tones would work well as graphic imagery for the walls, or maybe for a fun tablecloth and napkins.

Spend time on the details in this room. Source vintage books and stack them on the mantelpiece to create a focus.

Fun *flamingo fantasy*

Bright flamingo (**1**) could work equally well in a fun room for children or a grown-up bedroom or dressing room. Such saturated colours can appear, at first, to be rather naive, but mixed with sophisticated shades of porcelain and orchid, a whole new environment emerges.

Pink breathes joy and cheer into any area of the home.

Tinted porcelain greys (**2**, **3**) are the perfect accent colours for bright pink. These cool, neutral tones almost soak up some of the intensity of pinks. Use for clean, linear surfaces, such as tinted glass tabletops or armoire doors.

Sweet orchid (**4**) and deep purple (**5**) should be used as the detail colours in patterned textiles.

Add quirky elements, such as purple glass knobs on an old chest of drawers, or paint some old terracotta pots and fill them with flowers.

Lively, *cheeky and playful*

A cheerful, enlivening palette is not just for children.

Rosy pink (**1**) works best when mixed with cooler colours, such as blue or blue-biased greens. This powerful combination of colours would look great in a modern, lively kitchen; choose pink laminate for the cupboard doors and source lots of fun, colourful accessories.

1

2

3

4

5

True aqua or turquoise (**2**) is a strong colour to use anywhere in the home because it really draws in the eye. Use this in clever combination with a softer duck-egg blue (**3**) so that the mix of pink with blue does not become too harsh.

Lush, botanical lime greens (**4**, **5**) are fun accent colours. Source quirky plastic kitchen utensils, vibrant glazed ceramics and coloured glass bowls in lime colours so that practical items can be left on show.

Mix all five of these colours to create a colourful mosaic of wall tiles for around the sink and oven.

Romantic, *delicate pearl*

Carnation (**1**) works very well when mixed with natural tones of shell and pearl. Such an intense main colour in any room needs highlights that will soften the overall look. This is a great palette for a bedroom; accessorize with rose-tinted chandeliers, satin quilted throws and creamy, deep-pile carpets.

Heady pinks are perfect for a fragrant boudoir.

These accent colours are inspired by the soft, natural hues of giant seashells and mother-of-pearl. Try to find some accessories with shell or pearlized surfaces, such as coasters, jewellery boxes, small bowls or soap dishes. Vintage pieces can easily be found, but many modern outlets now produce good imitation pearlized trinkets.

For a special touch, mix pearlized glaze with delicate pink (**2**) and shell (**3**) for a shimmering paint surface.

Honey (**4**) and lichen (**5**) add some shadowy touches to this otherwise overly pretty palette.

Calm, *serene and tranquil*

Cool yet pretty colours are perfect for a modern bathroom.

This delightful lavender (**1**) is not too pretty and mixes well with modern hyacinth blue and fresh violet for an easy, striking palette. Consider the details in a bathroom; for example, invest in quality chrome fittings. Try bonded, coloured rubber instead of tiling on walls and floors.

Blues have been proven to evoke a calming feeling within a room. Violet (**2**) and cool hyacinth blue (**3**) will bring a sense of serenity to this pretty pink room. Use these tones on all woodwork in the room, including a panelled bath surround and bathroom cabinet.

Orchid (**5**) offers a sexy accent, preventing the room from becoming too cold. Use this for towels and a luxuriously textured bath mat.

Ice blue (**4**) is a wonderfully delicate tone that helps to balance the intensity of all the other colours, so use it for the flooring and shower curtain.

Eclectic, *contemporary, quirky*

Cotton candy (**1**) does not always have to be used in girly designs. Be bold when using strong colour combinations, such as pink with lemon and rose. Add a touch of the unexpected in the accent shades and see a very individual and modern environment unfold before your eyes.

A unique blend of natural and synthetic colours.

Use dusky rose (**2**) on woodwork and soft furnishings. Choose lightweight, translucent fabrics in buttery lemon (**3**) for delicate, sheer curtains.

Highlight colours are hugely important in this room, the sharper the colour the better. See the room come to life when the accent colours of turquoise and peach (**4, 5**) are given an injection of bright neon.

In order to further intensify the drama of this palette, choose materials such as glass or transparent plastic to enhance the accents, then direct light sources towards these objects.

Strawberry *chocolate fondant*

Sexy, strawberry pinks add a touch of indulgent glamour.

Strawberry mousse (**1**) could work equally well in a room with lots of natural daylight or in a romantic candlelit evening room, making it perfect for a bedroom. Accessorize with beaded cushions and floral tea-light holders. Let layers of rose-tinted muslin replace curtains or blinds.

Rich, expensive chocolates with sweet strawberry centres inspire these combinations for woodwork and accent colours. Use milk chocolate (**2**) for luxury leather and suede seating. Bitter chocolate (**3**) is perfect for window frames and deep skirting-boards.

For the truly daring, try using hot pink in the living area of the home. On romantic evenings, light candles and mocha-scented incense, and wrap up in cosy, pink cashmere sofa throws.

Collect kitsch accessories in bright, tones of raspberry fondant (**4**) and Turkish candy (**5**) for fun.

Charming, *languid and pleasing*

This palette of colours is at once peaceful and invigorating. Baby pink (**1**) is a lively colour to use in any interior. Combined with softened, lavender tones, a languid, relaxing atmosphere prevails. A sharp injection of bubble-gum pink offers a necessary boost of energy, which is so important in any modern room.

The perfect room for entertaining is energized with pink.

Baby pink (**1**), the main tone, matures when mixed with dusty plum (**2**) and powdery lavender (**3**) on woodwork. If a room painted entirely in pink seems too overpowering, try painting one wall or a recess area in one of these lowlight colours.

The final two accent colours in this room are opposite in terms of vibrancy and colour level. Bubble gum (**5**) is perfect for amusing accessories, such as cocktail glasses or risqué illustrations framed on the wall. Soft brown (**4**) is, in contrast, timid and soothing, perfectly rounding off this amiable palette.

Orchid, *hyacinth and violet*

An aromatic palette of florals from heather to lavender.

A medley of floral tones invokes a lush spring-garden ambience, perfect for a bathroom or a very feminine bedroom. Orchid (**1**) is enlivened with tonal shades of lavender and violet. By using scented candles and floral fabrics, you can create a greenhouse environment.

Sometimes using tones of the same colour is more interesting and has more impact than the use of contrasting shades. Strong colour can look less garish and much more designed when used in combination with paler tones of the same colour.

Heather colours (**2**, **3**) complement the pink tones of the main colour in the room. Use these for fine woodwork and soft chair covers.

Blue hyacinth shades (**4**, **5**) are heavier colours and must be used sparingly, but they offer real grounding to this flowery room.

Faded *antique porcelain*

Shell (**1**) is a delicate tint of pink that works well in a light and sunny living room or conservatory. The combination of soft and powdered pinks, greens and mauves is inspired by faded, vintage fabrics and antique, beaded handbags. Fill the room with flea-market and thrift-store finds, like overstuffed armchairs.

A perfect room for lazy afternoons of reading.

The success of this palette lies in the delicacy of the colours and the flat, almost greyed-off nature of the accents. Bring anything more pretty into this room and you instantly lose the air of elegance.

Use velvets and faded, woven fabrics in soft sage greens (**2**, **3**) to cover a selection of mismatched vintage armchairs, and to paint woodwork, including window frames and external doors.

These two graceful tones of dusty mauve (**4**, **5**) are perfect with the pink and greens. Mix all these tones in faded, floral fabrics for cushions or for covering old books.

Sensational, *sensual*

Show-stopping colour,
where accessories are
the star attractions.

Tinted pink porcelain (**1**) works so well in this room that it almost goes unnoticed. The perfect background colour is never overpowering, but simply frames the room's highlights. Take inspiration from art galleries, choose spectacular centrepieces and work the design around them.

Use peach-organza (**3**) voile layers as curtains at the windows, and to cover appliances, such as the television or bookshelves, that should not be on show.

Muted peach melba (**2**) can be used for wood-work details and floors, but keep everything very sleek and simple.

Source items that you simply love in poppy (**5**) or Japanese lacquered red (**4**), such as an antique silk kimono hung above the fireplace or a single, heavy piece of Murano glassware. You could also make a multitude of small-scale scatter cushions in shantung or moire silk using these red colours.

Flawless, *laundered and pure*

Painting any room in the home white, or off-white, makes it feel instantly clean, light and new. Prettier tones of sun-bleached pastel, like blush (**1**), are perfect for a bedroom or bathroom. Accessorize with French monogrammed towels and embroidered bed linen. Place dried lavender in the laundry basket for a fresh smell to match.

A mix of immaculate, tinted whites for a spotless finish.

1

2

3

The main accent colours in this room are very cool and calming. Choose pale dove (**2**) to paint the woodwork, including the bed frame and headboard, as well as the floorboards.

Hint of blue (**3**) should be used for furniture within the room since this colour is a happy partner to soft pink.

4

Dusky powder (**4**) and sunbeam (**5**) are the pretty elements in the room. Use in fine-striped linen to cover lampshades and cushions, or find oversized ceramic bowls to fill with soaps, silk flowers and shells.

5

Tuscan, *rustic and sun-kissed*

Sun-warmed tones are perfect for a country kitchen.

Tuscan pink (**1**) mixed with golden terracotta takes inspiration from the country houses of Tuscany in Italy, with their pale ochres and pasta yellows. These heirloom colours bring feelings of comfort into a kitchen. Accessorize with hand-thrown terracotta bowls filled with bread or lemons.

1

2

3

Use terracotta (**2**) for the floor tiles and work surfaces for a truly authentic, rustic look. Many DIY stores now stock real terracotta, or good imitation, tiles in a variety of shades.

Warm apricot (**3**) is the perfect country kitchen colour, evocative of fresh jam and pretty wild flowers. Use this colour for curtains and cushions on kitchen chairs, and to paint the door that leads to the kitchen garden.

4

5

Use rich cream (**4**) for the ceiling to give an impression of extra light. A darker level of cream (**5**) is used for plates and milk jugs.

Garden party, *floral fancy*

Rose (**1**) is so pretty it should almost come perfumed. It completes an ambrosial palette perfect for a bedroom or well-loved living space. Make this room as flowery as you like, or keep the surfaces simple and let the colours work their magic.

Combine English florals with pretty, flower-hued pinks.

Ivory (**2**) is to be used on all woodwork. Use either matt or gloss finish, depending on how rustic a look you want.

Stone (**3**) is a greened neutral that can be used to paint large pieces of furniture, such as armoires and chests of drawers. This soft neutral works as a fantastic backdrop to the medley of pinks around the room.

Peony (**4**) and snapdragon (**5**) are taken directly from the garden, and they look as pretty in striped and floral textiles as they do in fresh cut flowers.

Decorative *baroque elegance*

A rich palette needing extensive ornamentation.

Antique pink (**1**) is the perfect backdrop for displaying gorgeous objects. Take a grandiose attitude towards home interior design and source baroque-style decorative furniture and large-scale replicas of 16th-century European art. This palette is perfect for a decadent bathroom or living room.

Pale gold (**3**) shimmers and shines on sensuous curved surfaces. Use it in the details, perhaps on picture or mirror frames, to catch the light.

Paint furniture in rich cream (**2**) and hand decorate the edges with gold. You could also source swirled door handles and candelabra in gold.

Use deep blackberry (**5**) for the flooring and choose deep-pile carpets or rugs.

Plush velvet in Venus red (**4**) can be used to cover chair seats. Pick out a few special accessories in this hot colour, such as a glass vase or vintage perfume bottle.

Graphic, *urban and modern*

Coral (**1**) is taken in an unusually minimalist direction here. Neutral tones and cool teals are contrasting partners for a traditionally feminine colour. This contemporary palette is perfect for open-plan living spaces, since blocks of colour can be used in different areas, helping to segregate the environment.

Warm and cool tones in opposition inform an open-plan design.

Cement tones (**2**, **3**) can look fantastic when combined with vivid colour. Take inspiration from modern retail environments, and opt for polished, tinted concrete for flooring and internal support pillars.

Dusty blue (**4**) could be used for large, free-standing pieces of furniture, such as a sofa or chaise longue.

Choose a strong colour, such as teal (**5**), for kitchen surfaces. In an open-plan environment make a feature of the kitchen, rather than trying to conceal it with white.

Flowers *and mint*

A palette inspired by country wild flowers.

Sweet pea (**1**) is the perfect colour to bring pleasure and warmth into a bathroom, spare bedroom or garden room. Use this pink tone on only two or three of the walls since it may become too intense; break up the main colour with milk (**3**) or a pink-and-white striped wallpaper.

1

2

3

This sweet-pea mauve (**2**) is a perfect colour for embroidered flower details on towels or bed-covers and pillowcases. Paint a single wooden chair and cover the seat with floral fabric for the corner of the bathroom.

4

5

Mint (**4**) and thistle (**5**) greens are quite sharp accents perfect for glass or plastic products in the bathroom or bedroom. Use a fabric striped with both colours to cover a lampshade. Keep matching towels and fresh flowers in the guest bedroom, and leave sugared violets by the bed for a treat.

Theatrical, *dramatic cabaret*

Delicious, voluptuous pink (**1**) creates an instantly glamorous and provocative environment. Use heavy curtains in this room and keep the lighting low, preferably with candleholders on the walls instead of electric lights. Raise the bed onto a platform for a touch of added drama.

A decadent bedroom inspired by the Moulin Rouge.

Glossy black (**2**) looks fabulous for window frames, skirting-boards and doors. Paint decorative mirror frames to match. Choose black, curled wrought ironwork for the curtain rod.

Use deep purple (**3**) in lengths of lace for a new take on net curtains, or to make a seductive bedspread.

Slate green (**4**) or dusty green (**5**) are perfect for slinky silk bedcovers.

Go to town with accessories in this room: fill vases with long feathers and cover the bed in beaded scatter cushions.

Simple *picnic fun*

A bright and lively palette for indoor family picnics.

This over-the-top palette using fuchsia (**1**) is great for a fun family room. Keep walls and furniture simple with clean lines, then use fun accessories to get just the right look. Existing furniture, such as chairs, kitchen cupboards and picture frames, can be painted in bright tones.

The sunny, pale yellows (**2**, **3**) are perfect for bringing the feeling of natural daylight into the home.

Accessories in this room can be as kitsch and playful as you like. Choose brightly coloured plastics in sugar pink (**4**) and golden yellow (**5**) for plates and cutlery. These can be found with graphic floral or polka-dot prints.

Source a fun, multicoloured, striped tablecloth to use as a picnic blanket. For a children's party make lots of colourful food, like pink and yellow fairy cakes and pink lemonade.

Glowing, *radiant sunset*

Dense berry (**1**) needs luminous highlight colours to lift the room. Because this pink is so dark, it may make the room appear smaller – consider using pale peach (**3**) on one of the walls. Lighting is key here. You could even invest in a neon sign to hang on the wall.

Brilliant oranges complement this deep, crushed pink.

Pinky grey (**2**) will help to deflect the intensity of the other colours in the room. This elegant colour can be used for carpet and luxury suede furniture.

Pale peach (**3**) is a beautiful colour to use on woodwork in the room. Such a subtle hint of colour contrasts well with the main, darker colour.

Day-Glo peach (**4**) and sunset orange (**5**) can be used for coloured-glass light fixtures and ornaments. Source graphic-patterned fabrics in these colours for cushions.

Reds

Classic *and characteristic*

A strict palette for a Japanese-inspired room.

Nothing about this interior is accidental – everything has a place or a function. The definitive shapes are linear and simple with strictly measured dimensions. Furniture is black lacquered wood and the inspiration is traditional Japanese. This deep, rich wine (**1**) is perfect for an intimate, stylized dining area.

This room needs little decoration; it is more about clean surfaces and lines.

Parchment (**3**) is perfect for simple paper lampshades, and paper sliding partition doors; if possible find wax-covered paper or handmade paper for an authentic look.

Gold (**5**) is a wonderfully vibrant colour to use for chair cushions and small floor rugs.

Use a glossy, black lacquer (**2**) for high-backed chairs and a table, and red (**4**) for details, such as tassels and Japanese flowers.

Voluptuous *damson berry*

Port (**1**) comes from the blue-biased family of reds. When mixing with other red tones always marry from the same family, and stick to blue-biased or yellow-biased colours. Green is the opposing colour on the colour wheel, so it creates a dramatic contrast to red.

Sensuous, intense berry shades are not for the faint-hearted.

Aubergine (**2**) is a wonderful, darker version of the main colour, and it can be used on woodwork and flooring, either in carpets or dark, patina tiling.

Cyclamen (**3**) is also from the blue-biased family, so it works well in this scheme for furnishings. Cover a favourite old chair or sofa in cyclamen velvet for a practical yet fun focus in the room.

Chlorophyll (**4**) and brilliant turquoise (**5**) are opposite tones in this palette, creating a real vibrancy. Use these shocking hues for accessories, such as cushions, framed prints and fun glasses.

THE COLOUR PALETTE DIRECTORY

Earthy, *natural pigments*

Mineral colours inspired by real earth extracts.

The first paints ever made were from pigments, which are dyes taken from rock and earth colours. Ochre, sienna, umber and red earth (**1**) are natural colours that will give a restful feel to any environment. Natural paints are widely available so opt for toxin-free wall coatings.

1

2

3

Sand and stone (**2**, **3**) are very comfortable shades that can be used together for a discreet effect on woodwork and flooring, such as natural jute-woven matting. Using subtly different tones of the same colour is a clever way to mimic nature. Subtlety can often be just as arresting as a stark contrast.

4

5

Iron ore (**4**) and deep sienna (**5**) are basic, fundamental colours that offer rich and endless possibilities. Use these tones in natural fabrics such as linen or hemp. Accessorize with stone, earthenware and dark woods.

Positive, *cheerful and carefree*

True crimson (**1**) is one of the primary colours. In its purest form it can fill a room with joy and laughter. For an informal environment, such as a family room, or a fun open-plan kitchen for entertaining, this palette is wonderfully naive and instantly pleasing. Use hard-wearing, practical surfaces in this room.

Light-hearted colours that simply make you smile.

Dawn blue (**2**) is used on woodwork as an alternative to white. This pale tint offers a cool antidote to the powerful crimson walls.

Bluebell (**3**) is a great colour for plastics and other man-made materials. Choose ergonomically shaped seating and wipe-clean vinyl flooring.

Flame (**4**) and bright orange (**5**) are for cushions and utensils in the kitchen. Source playful plastic kitchen tools that children can use as easily as adults. Invest in a designer coat stand or a sleek, modern wall clock in resin or plastic.

Considered, *cool and careful*

A thoughtful use of contemplative colours for a study.

Muted but still vibrant, vermilion (**1**) has masculine undertones and needs refined, classic colours to complement it. A grown-up combination of cool greys and neutral blues offers a balanced palette of modern contrasts. Greys are smart, luxurious interior shades.

Neutral tones can be cool or warm. Historically viewed as drab or dreary, such natural colours are now being celebrated for their relaxing, comforting charm.

Natural stone (**2**) and rain cloud (**3**) are perfect cooling colours for this red. Use them for wooden or woven flooring and comfy reading chairs.

In fashion, this deep charcoal (**4**) is seen as a perfect alternative to black. Use in this scheme for around the fireplace, on picture frames, and bookshelves – practical and stylish.

A flash of blue (**5**) is a highlight for cushions and desktop accessories.

Soft, *feminine and pretty*

A delightful arrangement of pretty pale accents lifts this dusty roseate (**1**) colour. By opting for a softened or powdered red tone, the colour is rich but not overpowering. Colours are softened, yet seductive, and surfaces are matt.

Mellow colours with an antique finish.

Myrtle green (**2**) can be used for large, soft furnishings in this bedroom or sitting room. Use soft fabrics and loose covers for chairs and side tables.

Coral (**3**) can be used as a stain or antique tint for woodwork, cup-boards and armoires. Paint on one coat only and rub off excess paint to reveal some of the lovely natural wood beneath.

Pale peach (**4**) and panama hat (**5**) are perfect for decorative motifs and architectural features in the room. Use linen or 100 per cent cotton with natural textures running through the fabrics.

Moroccan, *sumptuous and spicy*

An indulgent, heady room filled with extravagant scents.

Hot, sultry and flushed, red rose petal (**1**) creates a lavish backdrop to a room meant for hedonistic indulgence. Highly flavoured and deeply decorated, this room is perfect for entertaining. Cover surfaces with candles in colourful Moroccan tea glasses.

Mulberry (**2**) is the secondary red tone in this room, further intensifying the grandeur. Use for traditional low seating, and mix with indigo and ruby silks from Morocco for scatter cushions and over-long curtains.

Mahogany (**3**) is used for the wood furniture and woodwork in this room, such as low tables and a fireplace.

Purple accent colours (**4**, **5**) are great for patterned fabrics. Also source coloured dishes and plates in which to serve the aromatic foods. Use coloured-glass lanterns for a subdued lighting.

Stimulate, *revive and rejuvenate*

Modern coral (**1**) is enlivening and warming, great for a bath- or shower room. Fresh and invigorating, this vibrating palette of reds and turquoises is a contrasting mix of brights. Even if every other room is calm and natural, go to town in a bathroom with colours that you simply love.

Dynamic colours are perfect for a wake-me-up bathroom.

Levels of bold turquoise blue (**2**, **3**) can be mixed together for tiling on the walls and floor – add a few random tiles in coral, too. Choose the paler of the two blues (**3**) for a plastic shower curtain and toilet-seat cover.

Violet (**4**) and neon pink (**5**) are modern highlights to be used sparingly and with a touch of humour. Source some kitsch, plastic accessories in these over-the-top shades.

Have a favourite phrase or mantra cut out in vinyl lettering to run around the walls of the room.

Shocking, *lively and confident*

A modern and bold palette, where neons work well with pales.

Shocking neon red (**1**) is great for a stairwell or dark area in your house; glowing undertones should be used in a hallway or area where people are moving around the house. Allow the colour to vibrate and work – do not mix with other bright reds since this will deaden the impact.

Softened pink colours (**2**, **3**) perfectly ground the vibrant main shade, preventing the room from becoming too frivolous. In direct contrast, the pinks can be used for subtly toned ceilings, skirting-boards and picture frames. Cover an old, buttoned chair in soft pink silk for a brilliant clash of antique with contemporary.

Flashes of lemon lime and neon yellow (**4**, **5**) would be perfect for lamps and lights. Look for a dramatic, overscaled 1960s light as a focus on the landing.

Cherries, *blossoms*

A wonderful cherry (**1**) tinged with coral and pink could easily work in both a traditional or modern interior. For cosy, indulgent evenings and fresh sunny days, combine this flourishing red with a mixture of pale and full accent tones. This is a clever, natural palette of blushing pinks and bud greens.

Bright, cherry red is relaxed with spring blossom colours.

Delicate blossom (**2**) is used on the woodwork, window frames and ornate ceiling features in a room with traditional details.

Soft baize green (**3**) is to be used for furnishings, rugs and curtains. Source prints and landscape paintings incorporating these types of greens.

Deep moss (**4**) and rose (**5**) are natural tones to accessorize this room. Go as simplistic or decorative as you like.

Search through antique shops for decorative tiles for the fireplace. Pinks and greens are typical of the art nouveau period invoked here.

Unrefined *adobe clay*

An intuitive palette of unspoiled shades and natural finishes.

Natural terracotta (**1**) and adobe colours make a great kitchen palette. These warm shades invoke a cosy, family environment. Use natural stone on the floor and scrubbed, antique pine furniture. An open fireplace would be great as the focus of the room.

Sun-bleached bone (**2**) is a very pale colour to be used in a family room, so use eggshell paint and waterproof fabric for chairs for a wipe-clean environment.

Pale pine (**3**) furniture is blocky and heavy for a lived-in quality.

Mud (**4**) and kidney bean (**5**) are lovely rustic shades, perfect for deep vegetable bowls, tiled work surfaces and your favourite leather chair by the fire.

These easygoing, relaxing colours are timeless. Invest in long-lasting furniture, and accessorize with new pictures and flowers when you feel like a change.

Jewelled, *precious scarlet*

Ruby, garnet (**1**), coral, jade, turquoise and emerald – this trinket box of opulent colours will enrich any room in the house. Experiment with new and different surface techniques, such as glazes and pearlized pigments, which further intensify the colours.

A treasure chest of rich colours needs no decoration.

These flame-coloured tones (**2**, **3**) are similar, but work together to exaggerate the depth of colour in this room. Use them together for glazed tabletops, cupboard doors or on a polished floor.

Pine-needle green (**5**) is a classic upholstery colour that could be brought up to date if used on modern furniture shapes.

Turquoise (**4**) is a wonderfully vibrant tone that can be used in shimmering fabrics for cushions and lamps with glass-beaded tassels.

For an unusual touch, create a feature on the wall with stick-on ruby rhinestones.

Fiery, *exotic and wild*

Flaming red walls are passionate and enticing.

The type of palette that could easily spill from inside out into the garden. Mix together shades of flame (**1**), pink and orange for the perfect summer party look. Imagine low seating, rugs, scatter cushions, sequined sari fabrics as curtains for patio doors and coloured glass lanterns.

This environment could be a haven for curiosities collected on foreign travels. Mix colourful Indian silks with classic Indonesian batik fabrics for cushions and curtains. Hang wind chimes in the trees and burn *nag champa* incense.

Mix and match these intense shades in contrasting patterns, textures and surfaces. Source a traditional Indian pagoda or large sun umbrella in these deep reds and oranges (**2**, **3**), dark ebony wood for furniture and magenta (**4**, **5**) silk for cushions.

Plush, *fine and jet set*

Deep ruby (**1**) alludes to a luxurious and expensive interior. These colours cry out for quality surfaces, such as plush, deep-pile carpets, soft leathers, polished lacquer tabletops and red Venetian glassware. Create a classical and refined room with plenty of details.

A palette inspired by the private jets of the rich and famous.

This palette could decorate a grand entrance hall, a dining area or a swish dressing room with concealed doors and underlit mirrors. Everything in this interior is tailor-made. For an alternative wall or floor covering why not go for soft leather panels?

Light cream and soft nubuck (**2**, **3**) are for leather seating and woodwork, contrasting with the ruby walls.

Black cherry (**4**) and navy (**5**) complete this quality mix; use on ostrich leather footstools, hand-crafted door handles and elegant glass lighting.

Aristocratic *pastoral*

Traditional country estates inspire this high-class palette.

Academy red (**1**), racing green and hunting brown were once colours reserved for English royalty. But today we can all enjoy these traditional shades. With the long tradition of handmade furniture and country living, this is a palette that will stand the test of time.

Colours of the land, forest (**2**) and fern (**3**) are perfect for furnishings and curtains. Choose heavy fabrics to exaggerate the feeling of luxury.

Pine cone (**4**) and chestnut (**5**) can be used for rich carpets and expensive-looking wooden furniture.

This room should be accessorized with paintings of traditional hunt scenes or vast landscapes. Source leather-bound books for bookshelves and an old-fashioned writing desk with a leather chair.

Composed, *restful and settled*

This is an unusually relaxing, rust (**1**) colour scheme that is perfect for historic properties, since it maintains a standard of authenticity. But don't confine such a great colour scheme to traditional environments. Take these natural tones into a modern living space and feel it become instantly cosy.

A dependable palette of rust red with rosy undertones.

This is a great palette for a kitchen or a dining or sitting room. The rich rust red background is an easy colour to work with, accepting many natural hues quite easily.

Brick (**2**) and hen's egg (**3**) are equally reliable tones, perfect for interior and exterior woodwork and flooring in wood, tiles or vinyl.

Straw (**4**) is a great colour for seating and curtains. In patterns or stripes, mix this colour with white for a fresh touch.

Sunny yellow (**5**) adds a touch of brightness in plates and teacups displayed in a cabinet or sideboard.

History, *heritage and heirlooms*

Spend time to reproduce a home's original style.

Make the most of the great variety of heritage paint colours on offer today, which instantly create an authentic atmosphere in an historic property. The naturally aged colours of worn and loved textiles enhance traditional rooms. Radicchio (**1**) is perfect for a study or living room.

1

2

3

The highlight colours in the room draw on historical reference, but are definitely not old-fashioned. Used cleverly and with more contemporary accessories and shapes, this palette can be brought up to date.

4

Rust (**2**) can be used for windows, photo frames and skirting-boards.

5

Ketchup (**3**) is a great colour for contemporary, bold furniture.

Army green (**4**) and air-force blue (**5**), common colours of the 1940s, are once again the height of fashion. Use military fabrics to cover cushions for a quirky alternative textile.

Afternoon tea: *antique tradition*

Claret (**1**) is softened with warm colours of petal peach and chiffon orange. Mid-tones of pinky mink help this quirky palette to blend. This room should be decorative, with floral fabrics and vintage plates hung on the walls. Revive the tradition of afternoon tea for a fun party with friends.

Delicious, dark claret red with tea-stained tones.

Deep red needs delicate colours to soften it. Use pinky mink (**3**) and copper blush (**2**) on different facets of the woodwork, creating graded stripes of colour. The warm, tinted neutral soaks up the rich red.

Use petal peach (**4**) and chiffon orange (**5**) for accessories. Source floral silk scarves to make into original, mismatched cushions. Use 1940s handbags, shoes, gloves or veiled hats to hang from picture frames and the mantelpiece.

Antique, floral porcelain tea sets are great to leave on the table. Fill with roses or old-fashioned sweets.

Oranges and Browns

Bitter chocolate, *sweet centres*

An irresistible blend of deep brown, mint and sugared violet.

Dark chocolate (**1**) is rich, but with red undertones, making it incredibly warming and welcoming in a room. It is perfect for a private haven, far from the hustle and bustle of everyday life. Such deep colours create a cocoon-like environment where you can indulge yourself in your own world.

Sugared violet (**3**) is a wonderfully delicate and pretty colour to use in conjunction with the sexy brown. Use this accent colour on woodwork, including any features such as dado rails, skirting-boards and a ceiling rose.

Pansy (**2**) is a dusty mauve, perfect for soft furnishings and big, feather-padded sofas and armchairs.

Use mint (**4**) and jade (**5**) to cool the palette. For a modern edge, use green glass for shelving in alcoves, and source an elegant green glass chandelier. Use green tiling around the fire, and green glass candlesticks on the mantle.

Mahogany, *chestnut and teak*

A natural palette inspired by the rich coloration of highly polished wood. Mahogany (**1**) is a deep-red wood colour. Choose this tone for walls in an elaborate, unusual bedroom environment. Mix with redwood furniture and accessories, such as a heavy four-poster bed and deep-framed paintings on the walls.

Rich auburn tones look wonderful with ginger and lemon.

Choose oatmeal (**2**) for natural woodwork, closet doors and wooden shutters at the windows.

Buttercup (**3**) is a strong, vibrant colour that adds a modern edge to this natural palette. Use this highlight colour for covering chairs and for curtains that the sun can naturally filter through.

These two shades of ginger (**4, 5**) are perfect for bedcovers and accessories. Mix textures on a bed with soft, satin duvet covers and cosy, fake-fur pillows. Stack old leather books by the bed with a simple brass lamp.

Toasted, *warming and cosy*

A glowing, burnished palette perfect for a lively kitchen.

This shade of toast (**1**) is wonderfully warming. A traditional colour is brought up to date when mixed with opulent purples and pinks. Suited to both traditional and modern environments, it's decadent on dark, winter evenings and luxurious in the summer months.

Such deep colour is not often found in a kitchen, but this palette is sure to delight both chef and dinner guests alike. Go for melt-in-the-mouth surface colours inspired by your favourite dishes, such as caramel pudding or tiramisu.

Use dusty plum (**3**) as the woodwork colour in this delicious room, a softened colour that complements both the pinks and the browns. Blackberry (**2**) is a great colour for kitchen cabinets.

Fuchsia (**4**) and coffee (**5**) can be used for accessories in the kitchen and matched to the soft furnishings.

Traditional, *historic folk shades*

A palette of natural pigments and dyes that have stood the test of time. Colours are created from the earth and fabrics are woven wool or animal skins. Spice (**1**) is a wonderfully earthy, fiery colour to have in a living or dining area.

A palette of folkloric colours inspired by the spice route.

Sienna (**2**) is a great colour for low, heavy furniture. Be influenced by the styles of Turkey with low seating and patterned rugs.

Henna (**3**) is a softened colour that can be used for curtains and large cushions in the room. Choose natural wool, linen and hemp fabrics.

Sandstone (**4**) and ivory (**5**) can be mixed with the other colours in traditional paisley or Ikat, an extraordinary silk fabric woven throughout Asia, for rugs, throws and wall hangings.

Teasing, *amusing and uplifting*

A joyful range of soft and light colours for bed or bath.

Have fun when choosing the colours for your home. Design is often taken far too seriously, so be bold and adventurous in your colour decision-making. Cinnamon punch (**1**) is a warming colour that is lifted and enlightened with tones of pink, ripe berry and mandarin.

Bubble gum (**2**) and pale rose (**3**) can be used for the woodwork, curtains and bedcovers. Choose a floral fabric for a pretty look, or opt for a simple stripe or polka dot for something quirky. Use the paler pink to paint floorboards, or for vinyl or laminated flooring in a bathroom.

Fabrics with dots or stripes in very berry (**4**) can be used as accents in the room. Use this colour to make small cushions for the bed.

Zingy mandarin (**5**) is a sharp accent that gives the whole room a lift. Use it on lampshades and drawer handles.

Persimmon: *ripe and fruity*

Persimmon (**1**) is a lush, orange-red fruit and a wonderful colour for a bedroom or family area. Use this tone with other fruit and berry colours for a rich yet mellow environment. In contrast, tinted, neutral tones help to season the palette, naturally balancing the colours.

A glorious palette of ripe fruit colours and soft, tinted neutrals.

Pomegranate-seed red (**3**) is a jewel of a colour – bright and glassy as the name suggests. Use this colour for rich leather seats and chairs, and elaborate glass vases or bowls filled with fruits and flowers.

Tinted grey (**2**) offers a great tone to soak up some of the juicy colours. Use this for woodwork and flooring, either a luxurious carpet or polished concrete.

Pink grapefruit (**4**) can be used for cushions and blinds for the window. Flowers in soft tea rose (**5**) make for a pretty room accent.

Architectural *and monumental*

Striking colours for a sweeping staircase or a grand entrance.

Strong burnt orange (**1**) can be an overpowering interior shade. Use this colour in an area where there is a lot of space, like a hall or stairwell. These colours are perfect for modern open-plan or double-height interiors, where colour can help to segregate sections of the space.

Steel (**2**) and dapple (**3**) are heavy greys that work well together. Use them in stripes with the burnt orange for curtains and furniture. Choose coated metal for picture frames and bannisters for an urban touch.

Lava (**4**) is a brash and overstated splash of colour to catch the eye. Use it in an open-plan area to colour a single piece of furniture. Alternatively, use it for the front door of the house, inside and out.

Cool blue (**5**) can be used for cupboard doors or as a painted square on the ceiling.

Bold, *powerful and melodramatic*

This is a fun combination of colours for a family bathroom. Red and orange traditionally clash, but the shades used here are similar enough to work together as highlights. Cool turquoise colours are a total contrast to marmalade (**1**), offering highs and lows of light and shade throughout the room.

Dramatic contrasts make for a lively environment.

Such contrasting combinations are bound to provoke an emotional response. Keep accessories and decoration to a minimum – the colours are already doing all the work needed.

Cool mint (**2**) and deep turquoise (**3**) are great colours for a shower curtain, and for stained glass at the window, in the cabinet door or in a light fixture.

Ruby (**4**) and blood orange (**5**) offer even hotter colours for items such as towels, plant pots and mirror frames.

Bashful, *shy and delicate*

Modest colours suited to a living room or conservatory.

These colours are reminiscent of a bygone era when ladies retired to their own room for activities such as needlepoint or poetry reading. Today such delicacies can be revived for a calm and meditative environment in the home. Use tangerine (**1**) alone or with the other colours in painted stripes.

Orange blossom (**2**) will probably be used in almost equal amounts to the main orange. This will maintain an air of sensitivity, so the orange does not overpower the rest of room.

Blond (**3**) can be used for pale wood furniture, wicker chairs and polished, pale wood flooring.

Mix these two quite similar shades of cool green (**4**, **5**) in a polka-dot fabric for seat cushions, curtains and fabric-covered lampshades.

Source antique china for afternoon tea with orange-blossom cakes and cucumber sandwiches.

Polka-dot *geometric*

These tones are inspired by the modern, geometric patterns of textiles and ceramics from the 1950s, when orange-juice (**1**) colours were mixed with lemon curd and outlined in black. Source original accessories for this room: hang a full-skirted dress above the fireplace or stack vinyl 45s on a side table.

Mix modern colours with original retro details.

Use cotton candy (**2**) for the woodwork in the room. Strawberry sorbet (**3**) is perfect for seat covers. Mix it with the main orange in polka-dot fabric patterns.

Lemon curd (**4**) is a great contrast colour in this room. Use it in details in a kitchen, such as on tea towels, breakfast bowls or even a bright toaster, juicer or coffee machine.

Black (**5**) is used as a linear motif throughout this design. All colours are mixed in retro ceramicware, Bakelite utensils and fun, original 1950s packaging tins left on show.

Peach *champagne cocktail*

A cocktail of contemporary colours, from soft to neon.

Peach champagne (**1**) is combined with steely greys and neon fuchsia. In true eclectic style we have mixed and matched our inspirations and come up with a very modern look. Use this palette in a bedroom, bathroom or even a study with lots of glass and natural light.

Steel (**2**) can be used for super-soft velvet chairs and sofas. Paint the woodwork and floor with pale iced blue (**3**) and use steel-coloured sheepskin rugs as an alternative to carpet in the bedroom or bathroom. In a study use the iced blue as a calming element by painting the desk and bookshelves.

Good quality cotton in rich fuchsia (**4**) can be used for bedding. Accent this with contrasting satin cushions.

Use the neon pink (**5**) for lighting, fun pen or toothbrush holders, and for drawer handles.

Gentle, *whitened and light*

A wonderfully pale combination of colours is accented with a sharp injection of true orange. This contrasting use of colours brings out the tones of the main shade, nectar (**1**). Use this palette in a bedroom or kitchen for a feminine, yet modern take on pastels.

Softened pastel colours for a soothing, mild environment.

1

2

3

Summer-sky blue (**2**) is a fresh and uplifting colour to be used for soft furnishings and carpets.

Tranquil green (**3**) can be used in flat paint for woodwork, kitchen cupboards and any external doors in the room.

4

Dusky lavender (**4**) is less clean than the other colours in the room. It is a great shade for heavy wovens or sueded fabric to cover chairs.

5

Use bold signal orange (**5**) in prints on the walls or in patterned cushions and ceramic bowls.

Dusty, *faded and matt*

Drama can be found in almost colourless colours.

A very clever use of colours – it takes real confidence to opt for a palette where the colours are pale and washed out. Subtle use of colour can easily be as dramatic as bold combinations. Mix textures and surfaces in this room to enhance the delicate peaches and cream (**1**) shades.

Dusty mauve (**2**) and sugared almond (**3**) are pretty, antiqued colours, perfect for jacquard fabrics on chairs and cushions. Choose regency-inspired, swirling patterns in combinations of light and shade.

Pistachio ice cream (**4**) is the perfect shade for painted floorboards, window shutters and sills, and skirting-boards.

Choose pale khaki (**5**) to mix with the other colours for fabric patterns or for a single area of wallpaper. It can be a great focus in a room to simply paper a chimney breast in a bold, floral or geometric pattern.

Orange cream *and sweet balm*

Sweet orange mousse (**1**) could be taken into a totally feminine palette, but here it is used in a traditional range based on natural hues and historic colour combinations. Delicate lemon and soft, deep browns mix together to create a cosy country kitchen that easily translates into 21st-century style.

Kitchen colours scented with orange and lemon balm.

Toffee (**2**) and butterscotch (**3**) are rich, homely colours perfectly suited to the cooking environment. Use them in the form of orange-hued woods, such as cherry or beech, for kitchen cupboards or an informal scrubbed dining table and chairs.

Lemon meringue (**4**) is a light and fluffy colour perfect for lace curtains and feather-filled chair cushions.

Use deep ebony (**5**) for the stone or wood flooring for an elegant but practical finish. Complete the look with fruit and serving bowls carved from dark wood.

Natural *oranges and blues*

Striking natural pigments from earth tones to lapis lazuli.

Brick (**1**) is a natural complement to blue. Painters once had to source natural pigments and mix their own paints. Lapis lazuli came from Afghanistan and was more expensive than gold. It produced the most brilliant of blues and was made famous by the Venetian artist Titian.

This palette would work well in a bathroom, kitchen or dining room. Use traditional Moroccan tadelakt, a lime-based, water-resistant plaster, on the walls.

Use a darker terracotta (**2**) for the natural baked tile flooring. Rich, Turkish red (**3**) is perfect for kitchen cupboards and wood.

Intense blues like cobalt and lapis lazuli (**4**, **5**) are perfect for heavy, woven fabrics for curtains and seat covers. Source tiles with the traditional, rich blue patterning from Africa or Andalusia for an authentic look.

Delicious, *luxurious and sensual*

This is an incredibly sexy palette and could work just as well in a living room as in a bedroom. Irresistible shades of caramel (**1**), hot chocolate and chestnut are enlivened with rich, succulent injections of plum and purple suede. Use good quality materials in this room.

Rich coloration ensures a seductive environment.

Use the softest and most luxurious surfaces in here, such as matt, powdery paint finishes for the walls. Cashmere, suede and velvet are perfect indulgences to mix and match for furniture, curtains and cushions. Invest in fine touches, such as hand-blocked wallpaper on one wall or an oversized antique mirror above the fireplace.

Use the chocolate shades (**2**, **3**) for heavy furniture and period details in the room. Plum (**4**) and purple fig (**5**) are wonderful shades for fabrics and glassware.

Linear *and well designed*

Unobtrusive colours perfect for clean, modern designs.

This is a clean, simple style reminiscent of the 1950s. Walnut (**1**) is perfect for a stylized dining room. When using drab colours, design ethics have to be strict for the palette to work. As designer and poet William Morris said, 'have nothing in your houses that you do not know to be useful or believe to be beautiful'.

Fabrics should be linen with a texture running through the weave. Source original one-off furniture pieces in cherry wood to coordinate.

These similar shades of straw (**2**, **3**) are perfect to use in stripes for fabrics. Also, use the paler of the two colours for woodwork and door frames.

Soft khaki (**4**) is the darkest shade within the room. Use it for the carpet and large seat covers.

Putty (**5**) is a great tinted neutral. Mix it with the other colours in 1950s-style furnishing fabrics or in original paperback books.

Masculine, *chic and smart*

Source traditional suit fabrics, such as tweed, herringbone and even Scottish tartan, for an alternative material to cover seats and sofas. Use these natural wools to inspire the colour scheme for the room. Saffron (**1**) is a sophisticated, natural foundation on which to build this palette.

A formal palette inspired by gentlemen's tailors.

This palette would work well in a study or living–dining area. The colours are smart and tailored, but the bold saffron orange offers a sense of fun.

Bark (**2**) and bracken (**3**) are wonderfully deep, natural colorations, perfect for furniture, deep skirting-boards and around fireplaces.

Air-force blue (**4**) is a cool accent among these warm shades. Mix it in the weave for fabrics and furnishings, or use it for picture frames.

Turmeric (**5**) is a bright highlight that can be used for corduroy cushions and light fixtures.

Sweet icing *and sugared almonds*

Harmonious sugar-coated pastels subdue hot orange.

Hot candied peel (**1**) is mellowed slightly with a flat, whitened finish, so use eggshell paint and natural fabrics to soften the impact of the bold colour. These aromatic colours are washed out to prevent the room from becoming sharp or sickly.

Soft pistachio (**3**) is perfect for a contrast colour on woodwork. If the green is too contrasted, white will lighten the overall feel. Use white on the woodwork, and mix it in stripes or checks with the pistachio and dusty mauve (**2**) for fabrics, furnishings and carpets. This palette could work well in a bedroom or living room.

Peach and toffee (**4, 5**) are great colours for details. Use on light fixtures, candlesticks and bowls for fruit, jewellery or flowers.

Mix *cosmopolitan with country*

A bold and modern palette that could work well in a new or old building and is perfect for a contemporary yet practical kitchen space or a rustic country bedroom. Ginger (**1**) gives a homely feel to any room, and mixing it with peony pinks breaks away from the traditional terracotta and yellow combination.

Warm and cool colours contrast for a rustic yet modern look.

Two shades of peony (**2**, **3**) are wonderfully rich and decorative colours that look great as blocks of flat colour on kitchen cupboards or surfaces. Mix them with the cool shades below on modern florals or graphic printed fabrics.

Porcelain tint (**5**) and ice blue (**4**) bring contrast to the palette. These cool colours help to prevent this room from becoming too pretty or too traditional.

Go for a mixture of accessories from worn and loved, faded armchairs to modern glass shelving and lampshades.

Coffee *and after-dinner mint*

A dining room for entertaining should be elegant but fun.

The finest shades of coffee (**1**) and chocolate are perfect for any dining area. Exquisitely rich and instantly gratifying, brown tones create a feeling of warmth in any room. Accessorize with quirky dinner plates in bright mint and cutlery made from fake tortoiseshell or polished coconut.

Espresso (**2**) is a darker version of the main colour. Use it for the woodwork and dining table. For an unusual touch, paint vertical stripes of espresso with fudge (**3**) along the length of the table.

Use bright mint (**4**) and mint (**5**) in fabrics for chair seats and curtains. For a modern fireplace, use mint tiles. Source recycled green glass tumblers and goblets.

Serve mint martinis or mint tea with fresh mint leaves, and make mint chocolate mousse in green Moroccan tea glasses.

Nutmeg, *tea and pumpkin*

When designing any environment, you must take into account all five senses. Colours can stimulate us visually, but use scents of cinnamon and nutmeg (**1**) or freshly-baked pumpkin pie for a complementing scent and taste sensation. Search for fabrics that demand to be stroked and play uplifting music.

A stimulating palette that arouses all the senses.

Rich nutmeg (**1**) is a sexy base colour upon which to build a palette. These colours would transform a tired kitchen or dining area.

Aqua (**2**) and robin's-egg blue (**3**) both offer a bright and softened accent. Use them in varying degrees depending on your taste for intense colours.

Honey (**4**) can be used for curtains and picture or mirror frames. Mix honey with robin's egg and amber (**5**) in fine-striped fabrics for seat covers, cushions, and quirky teacups and plates.

Chestnut *and saddle*

A traditional brown is enlivened with hot flame colours.

The classic colour of leather (**1**) is underappreciated in interior design. This rich and expensive-looking shade is incredibly versatile. Mix it with simple, neutral shades for a timeless, conservative look, or use bright accents for a modern edge.

Café latte (**2**) and coffee cream (**3**) are perfect accent shades, blending easily with the main colour. Use these warm, creamy tones on woodwork and fabrics, such as suedes and leathers, for upholstery. Mix these colours in an ice-cream swirl for contemporary, cast-resin furniture, such as tables and side chairs.

Many modern accent colours would work here, such as violet or turquoise. Flame red and flame orange (**4**, **5**) offer a spicy touch. Utilize these colours in accessories such as cushions and lampshades in Chinese silk.

Elegant, *understated neutrals*

Rich tea (**1**) is beautifully complemented by these soft tints of powdered heritage colours, making the new neutrals very elegant. This deeply luxurious palette is perfect for a sensuous boudoir or a wonderfully indulgent bathroom. Use a soft, pinked tone on the wall behind the bed to lift the dark brown.

Tinted natural shades enhance this rich, deep brown.

Soft pink (**2**) is the main accent colour and can be used almost as much as the tea (**1**). Use it in a flat finish on the walls and contrast in high gloss for the woodwork and for wood panelling in a bathroom.

The soft browns (**3**, **4**, **5**) are pretty yet sophisticated. Use for satin cushions, a tinted glass chandelier and mismatched bowls.

Accessorize with decorative, antique, French-style furniture and monogrammed bed linen and towels. Use an old, curved, wrought-iron garden chair for seating.

Yellows

Seasoned, *masculine and polish*

A palette for a gentleman's study or sitting room.

These easy tan colours are inviting and relaxing. A sophisticated palette of golden ochre (**1**) and warm, natural colours is perfect for a workroom or study area. Look to surfaces used in museums and libraries, such as wood panelling, buttoned leather and even linen wallcoverings.

Rich, golden ochre is softened with muted accent colours for a luxurious feel. For a quality finish choose natural paints made from traditional earth pigments. These paints will last a long time and have a milder odour compared to their chemical counterparts.

Straw (**2**) and string (**3**) are versatile colours that offer a true classic finish.

Chestnut (**4**) is a perfect colour for leather chairs and a leather-covered writing desk. Mix straw, string and sand (**5**) in textiles for a floor rug and heavy velvet curtains. Cover a single area of the wall with natural linen wallpaper.

Ripened *country corn*

Tones of ripened corn (**1**) evoke long summer days and warm evenings. Such natural colours are perfect for country houses, cottages and older character buildings. These yellows would also work well on the exterior of a house. Use them for a cosy kitchen or conservatory.

Rich, egg-yolk yellows inspire a warm ambience.

Choosing yellows with a warm, orange glow gives a soft touch and invokes a comfortable ambience.

Dark forest green (**2**) is a classic colour to combine with ochre tones. Think of old-fashioned racing cars with corn (**3**) leather seating when choosing the furniture. Use forest green for a traditional farmhouse oven and for cupboard doors.

Egg yolk (**4**) and ginger (**5**) are great cooking colours to have in the kitchen, and are also natural and practical for accessories.

Bold, *desert neutrals*

Tinted neutrals and acid brights are modern and graphic.

Neutral tones are incredibly versatile. Choose a good neutral base and you can keep the colour on the walls for many years – simply change the accent colours to create a totally new space with little added expense. Desert (**1**) works just as well with terracottas or soft greens.

Modern interior decorating is all about clever use of colour. This does not mean that we all have to go for vibrant pigments. It has become the height of contemporary interior design fashion to choose beautiful, tinted neutral tones throughout the house.

Rabbit (**2**) and warm grey (**3**) are subtle colours that work well because they have a warm glow to them.

To keep the room from becoming drab, acid lime (**4**) is used sparingly on fabric patterns and accessories. Slate (**5**) gives a dark outline for details and finishes.

A Côte d'Azur *tanned classic*

Beach sand (**1**), bronzed bodies and the azure ocean create a perfectly harmonious palette. This classic yellow tone is given a new direction with clever use of colour in the accessories and woodwork. Brown and azure always look good together, be it in interior design or fashion.

Inspired by the colours of the Mediterranean.

The secondary colours of tan (**2**) and chestnut brown (**3**) give richness to the main yellow. This palette would work well in a living or dining area with 1950s-style wooden furniture in walnut or cherry.

Dusty green (**4**) and azure (**5**) are wonderful accessory colours for velvet cushions and gorgeous ceramics.

When looking for fabric for the interior be inventive. Visit tailors instead of upholsterers to source traditional tweeds and wools for covering chairs.

Sunshine *play*

Use primary colours in a fun room for family and friends.

This vibrant sunshine yellow (**1**) is fun and enlivening. Such a clean primary colour can be used for a children's play area or any room used for entertaining. With accents of ice-cream colours and primary blues, this palette utilizes opposing cool and warm tones.

Choose vanilla ice cream (**2**) for the woodwork, and for one of the walls if you do not want the yellow to overpower the space.

Raspberry ripple (**3**) is a fantastic colour for plastic chairs or fun beanbag chairs. Any upholstery and flooring in this room should be easy to clean as there will be a lot of traffic passing through.

Elementary blues such as navy (**5**) and china blue (**4**) are perfect partners to rich yellow. Use them for cushions, curtains and wooden storage crates to tidy away all the children's toys.

Spring crocus *and cowslips*

These colours would be perfect to wake up to in the morning. Lemon cake (**1**) is sweet and charming while daybreak tones of sunlight yellow and new-shoot green are fresh and uplifting. Utilize this palette in a bedroom, bathroom or kitchen for an instant morning glow.

A light and airy palette inspired by spring meadows.

1

2

3

Pretty ivory (**2**) is a perfect colour for curtains and will let the morning rays of sun filter into the room naturally. Use this colour for woodwork and even on painted floorboards to increase the lightness of the room.

Sprightly mint (**3**) is a really fresh green. Paint it over wooden furniture such as chairs and cupboards. Alternatively, choose it for breakfast plates in the kitchen.

4

5

Fern green (**4**) and peach (**5**) can be used for delicate, floral prints or embroidery on bed linen, towels or upholstery fabrics.

Honey *and vanilla cream*

Sweet and sensuous pastry colours are richly indulgent.

A delectable colour palette of honey (**1**), rich vanilla cream and hot chocolate is brought up to date when accessorized with intense and sensuous raspberry and neon pink. This palette would work well in a living room or bedroom; it is classic yet fun.

1

2

3

The main colours in this room of honey (**1**) and cream (**2**) are simply elegant.

Chocolate brown (**3**) is no longer a colour for traditionalists. Use this rich tone for the floors and for modern, low tables. Fabrics can be chocolate with graphic prints in bright pink mixed with cream. In the bedroom why not try a chocolate, fake-fur throw on the bed?

4

5

Choose raspberry (**4**) and neon pink (**5**) for eye-catching accessories, such as a single designer chair or dark pink roses in cream ceramic vases.

Diverse, *neat and tidy*

This unconventional colour combination works well because of the washed-out, or dusty, quality of the main colours. The main faded buttercup (**1**) is the type of colour that could really work throughout the home. It is neutral enough to make a perfect background, yet energetic enough to create atmosphere.

A strong mix of colours needs a lack of clutter.

Pale lilac (**2**) and cool amethyst (**3**) are tints of colour that perfectly balance with the main buttercup tone. Use these shades for floors and large pieces of furniture.

Muted yellow (**4**) and mandarin (**5**) offer brighter highlights within the room while still complementing the main shade.

Mix all the highlight colours together in quirky, Chanel-inspired, textured, woven fabrics for chairs and sofas.

A sunny *rose garden*

This modern vintage feel is all about the feminine details.

A bright, sunny bathroom in pretty yellow rose (**1**) is perfectly accessorized in colours from the rose garden. Choose reclaimed furniture for this room: a traditional free-standing bath, original fittings and stripped wooden chairs and cabinets. Surfaces have a flat, faded finish.

Light khaki (**2**) and pistachio (**3**) are perfect colours for a flat wood-work finish. Wooden panelling in the bathroom can be painted the same colour as the cupboards, window frames and towel rails.

Cover an old chair with striped fabric in rose (**4**) and geranium (**5**), and use the same fabric for curtains and tiebacks.

Accessorize with a reproduction ceramic floral soap dish and water jug for a vintage feel. You could also source pink glycerine soaps and bath products with floral fragrances.

Salon *star treatment*

Choose surfaces carefully, and contrast glossy and smooth textures to exaggerate soft lemon (**1**) tints. With well-chosen French-style furniture and accessories, you could create a real salon feel. Lots of light is needed in this room at all times of day in order to differentiate between the colours.

A delightful medley of pastels creates a soft, pretty mood.

1

2

3

Flat, lemon yellow walls are challenged when set against the lacquered finish of mint (**2**) and soft sage green (**3**) for glossy woodwork and shelving.

Use pale pink (**4**) and soft peach (**5**) velvet for quilting. Sheepskin and sequinned cushions add depth, luxury and texture. Hang a sparkly chandelier in this room for a truly decadent salon experience.

4

5

For a totally glamorous approach, look for a pink- or peach-tinted mirror to use as a tabletop or, alternatively, frame it with dressing-room light bulbs and hang it for that superstar treatment.

Subtle, *cool and relaxing*

Stylish, refined colours for a dining room or work area.

Natural wheat (**1**) is great for plain walls or for painting over textured wallpaper, such as woven fabric or fine, vertical, textured stripes. This palette of soft yellow, white and cool blue grey is a modern, paler interpretation of a traditional interior look. It invokes a calming and hospitable atmosphere.

1

2

3

You may say that white (**2**) is not a colour, but here we are using white woodwork as a partner to soft yellow to keep the look clean and graphic.

Pale, dusty blue (**3**) is a fantastic colour for upholstery. Choose a textured fabric such as velvet, heavy wovens or even knitted surfaces for an unusual touch.

4

5

Modern accessories in slate blue (**4**) and gun-metal grey (**5**) should have simple shapes with minimal decoration. Choose square, Japanese-style dining plates and narrow, extra-tall vases to stand out against the pale yellow walls.

Cosmetic *cream and powder*

Cream (**1**) is often a prettier alternative to pure white, and here it is mixed in a delicious blend with skin tones of peach sorbet, butterscotch and rose pink. Deliciously feminine and aromatic, these tones could be used in almost any combination. It is a perfect palette for the bedroom that works just as well in the kitchen.

A palette inspired by fragrant make-up.

1

2

3

Just like applying make-up, build the layers of this room gradually until the perfect finish is achieved.

Pressed powder (**2**) and sweet biscuit (**3**) are great foundation colours. Use these feminine neutrals for the flooring and bed-covers; in the kitchen paint the cabinets in a flat or eggshell finish.

Blush pink (**4**) can be used for selected fabric embellishment.

4

5

Rich butterscotch (**5**) is a strong colour and must be used sparingly, perhaps only on cupboard handles and glassware.

Hints of lemon; *lush, graphic*

Fresh lemon and rich mid-tones in a luxurious blend.

Citrus (**1**) is a lime-based tinted yellow and the perfect ground for a lush palette of fern greens and orchid mauves. Use the main colour and the two green accent tones to complement each other, like shadows, in alcoves and on the chimney breast. This pretty palette could work in any room.

1

2

3

Limeade (**2**) and fern (**3**) are perfect yellow-based greens. By cleverly combining these two different depths of colour with the main colour, a contemporary and graphic look can be achieved. Always use masking tape when painting different colours next to each other in order to maintain sharp lines.

4

5

Use the pretty tones of orchid (**4**) and sweet pea (**5**) in striped fabrics for curtains and cushions. Source tropical orchids in similar colours, and place three identical plants in the centre of a low table for a sleek finish.

Sherbet: *zingy and sparkling*

This super-pale, lemon sherbet (**1**) is light and airy, giving a zesty lift to any tired bedroom or bathroom. Use it to breathe new life into dark areas and rooms that do not get a lot of daylight. Yellow and blue is a classic yet exhilarating combination. Consider glitter paints for details.

A classic colour combination with a light twist.

These blues have been carefully selected for a clean, fresh feeling. Bright aqua (**3**) and Wedgwood blue (**2**) are at quite different ends of the blue scale, yet sit happily together with the sherbet. Use the blues for woodwork and to match tiling in a bathroom.

The accent colours in this palette are soft and in contrast with the brighter main colours. By accessorizing in greyed shades of blue, the overall look of the room does not become too naive or kitsch. Use duck egg (**4**) and soft clay (**5**) for fabrics and fixtures.

Hot *Indian summer*

Fiery colours create a hot Bollywood experience.

Yellow gold (**1**) is combined with a range of super-hot oranges for a glowing palette inspired by Bollywood. Vibrant, expressive and fun, this palette can either be used as inspiration, or taken to a fully themed environment with sari curtains and glitzy details.

Use sunset orange (**3**) and peach puff (**2**) for tinted Formica surfaces on tabletops.

For a really kitsch touch, have a collection of Bollywood film posters printed onto Formica and use them for tabletop surfaces.

Transparent, traditional Indian sari fabrics in hot marigold (**4**) are perfect as an alternative to curtains and for cushion covers. Source garlands of paper flowers to drape from the curtain rods and over the mantelpiece.

Fill deep glass bowls in rich aubergine (**5**) with brightly coloured traditional Indian sweets.

Whimsical, *mystical shimmer*

Shimmering lily (**1**) is almost dreamlike in its ethereal quality. Such a pale and fragile colour will lift any room, giving it a light and dreamy atmosphere. Mix with a palette of dragonfly greens and deep-forest violets for a fantasy bathroom perfect for long, secret baths.

Surreal contrasts of lemon and green for a fairy-tale bathroom.

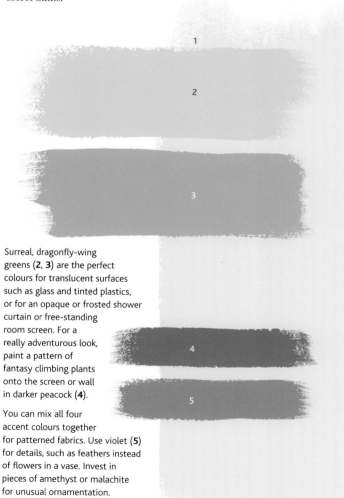

Surreal, dragonfly-wing greens (**2, 3**) are the perfect colours for translucent surfaces such as glass and tinted plastics, or for an opaque or frosted shower curtain or free-standing room screen. For a really adventurous look, paint a pattern of fantasy climbing plants onto the screen or wall in darker peacock (**4**).

You can mix all four accent colours together for patterned fabrics. Use violet (**5**) for details, such as feathers instead of flowers in a vase. Invest in pieces of amethyst or malachite for unusual ornamentation.

Clear, *fresh and energetic*

Revitalizing colours that almost take your breath away.

Mix brilliant crayon yellow (**1**) with active blues and spearmint for a dynamic palette, great for any lively room. You can make use of artificial colours just as often as naturally influenced tones, and such vivid, modern paints should be celebrated for their totally contemporary appeal.

1

2

3

Lime (**3**) is the perfect partner to the main bright yellow and can be mixed with white in stripes if desired. Spearmint (**2**) is a softer, yet equally animated colour that can be used for floors and woodwork.

4

5

Clean turquoise (**4**) is great for a fun children's bedroom or play area. Use it for plastic seating or for the bedframe.

Cornflower blue (**5**) is traditionally a favourite colour for a boy's room. Mixed with these other fresh colours, cornflower becomes a graphic accent colour useful for picture frames. Try painting racing stripes around the room.

Light and lavish *lime*

This luminous palette of lime yellow (**1**) and rich, botanical jungle greens would make an intense and decadent living space. If possible, choose a room that opens directly onto the garden. Greened tones are layered from soft pea through to deep olive.

Succulent mouth-watering limes and overgrown greens.

Deepest olive (**2**) is a luscious colour to use in combination with lime yellow (**1**) on glossy woodwork in a living room. Paint wooden blinds at the windows for a colonial style.

Paradise pink (**3**) is a much needed respite from all the green in the room. Use it in fabric patterns and for fruit bowls and dinner and side plates.

Electric limes (**4**, **5**) should be used sparingly in fabrics and on lampshades.

Mix the colours together in retro-style, giant, floral-patterned fabrics for a kitsch touch on cushions and covered footstools.

Art deco: *classic good taste*

Use historical colour references for a touch of instant style.

Putty (**1**) is typical of some of the first interior paint colours produced in the early 20th century. A classic colour, it works equally well in a period property or a modern, open-plan space. Accessorize with geometric chrome on kitchen appliances and table and chair legs.

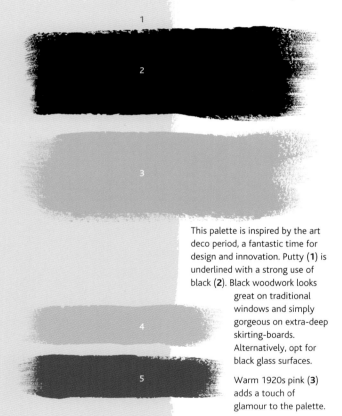

This palette is inspired by the art deco period, a fantastic time for design and innovation. Putty (**1**) is underlined with a strong use of black (**2**). Black woodwork looks great on traditional windows and simply gorgeous on extra-deep skirting-boards. Alternatively, opt for black glass surfaces.

Warm 1920s pink (**3**) adds a touch of glamour to the palette.

Nile green (**4**) was the epitome of fashion during this period. Use with nut brown (**5**) in furnishings and details to complete this look. Source original art deco furniture and authentic textile prints.

Bamboo *and chinoiserie style*

Bamboo (**1**) is used all over the world for making furniture, flooring and lightweight utensils; it also grows quickly and is environmentally friendly. The subtle tones of bamboo make the perfect inspiration for a warm background colour. Be inspired by the influence of Chinese art on early 19th-century interiors.

Earthy pigments and finishings create an Eastern look.

Intense lacquered red (**2**) can be varnished or glazed after painting to recreate the traditional Chinese finish to woodwork. Use for doors and oversized wooden cupboards or armoires. Source heavy, unpolished brass knobs and handles for an authentic feel, and accessorize with red or yellow silk tassels.

Brick red (**3**) is the perfect colour for fabrics. Choose either decorative Chinese jacquards or plain velvet.

Rich earth (**4**) and lucky yellow (**5**) can be used in Chinese-style patterns and ornaments.

Girly, *mischievous, flirtatious*

Flirt with colour in a mix of tongue-in-cheek brights.

Decorating your home should be enjoyable so really let your personality shine through in the colours you choose. Natural, fruity colours like pear (**1**) always make people smile. Let rooms in your home become an extension of your wardrobe by filling them with favourite colours.

1

2

3

Flamboyant floral colours mix easily in a happy room. Choose lemon-lime meringue (**2**) for the woodwork, doors and ceiling coving to soften the edges of this lively environment.

Leaf green (**3**) could be used to paint furniture, such as kitchen chairs or cupboard doors.

4

5

Use bubble gum (**5**) and jawbreaker (**4**) as candy colours for seat covers. Find funky kitchen accessories, like rubber gloves, tea towels and a broom and dustpan to hang on the wall, in these bright shades.

Camomile *infusion*

Camomile (**1**) gets a classic finish when combined with tea browns. This palette works in a living room, dining area or open-plan kitchen. Warmed colours melt together to create an instantly cosy atmosphere perfect for sunny mornings or winter evenings around the fire.

Cuddle up in warm, comforting tones of yellow and tea.

1

2

3

Tea (**2**) is the major secondary colour. Use it for the flooring and a large, family dining table.

Wholemeal (**3**) is a rather sophisticated colour, but it adds a needed element of neutrality to curtains and work surfaces.

4

Accessorize with battered, old leather armchairs and hand-knitted blankets or patchwork throws. Stack chopped firewood in an unused grate or along the wall as a feature.

5

Use tobacco (**4**) and begonia (**5**) in fabrics and hand-painted ceramics.

Illustrative, *off-beat and visual*

A computer-generated palette for modern interiors.

A contrasting palette of lights and darks that is inspired by modern graphic illustration. Look for nightclub flyers or business cards from trendy shops and imitate their contemporary use of muted colour with flashes of highlight. Willow (**1**) is a safe colour on which to build this unpredictable scheme.

Natural colours are improved upon here with man-made techniques. Dusky rose (**2**) and jungle (**3**) are richer, sharper versions of their natural origins. Use jungle for the woodwork and dusky rose for flooring and designer furniture.

Garnet (**4**) is the all-important underlining colour in this room. Use in graphic patterns on wallpaper, cushions, serving plates and wall posters.

Use sunset orange (**5**) for modern lighting and an entertainment centre that hangs on the wall like a painting.

Sun-ripened *Nordic blond*

This classic range of colours is inspired by Scandinavian landscapes. Northern light makes colours look cool and clear, and these countries are historically more likely to opt for cool interior shades. Great for a kitchen or bathroom, blond (**1**) and blue are basic shades with a twist.

Everyday colours for a lively yet restorative palette.

Blond (**1**) can be used in fabric wallcoverings or painted over textured paper.

Corn (**2**) is a cleaner, more primary yellow to be used for the window frames and will exaggerate any sunlight that filters through. Use pea green (**3**) for kitchen cupboards and bathroom cabinets.

Teal (**4**) and petrol blue (**5**) are perfect for furnishing fabrics. Choose corduroy for seat covers and pick curtains with unusual textures.

Source Nordic landscape paintings to tie the colour scheme together.

Greens

Natural, *balanced forest*

Mix light and dark greens to restore a room's equilibrium.

Green is the colour in the centre of the rainbow and the colour wheel, and for this reason it is said to be a balancing colour. The colour of nature, the forest (**1**) and new growth, green is also a restorative colour that can lift the spirit. Use green in a dining area to create a comfortable yet invigorating environment.

1

2

3

If dark green is the predominant colour in a room, you will need to have pale shades to prevent the room from becoming too overbearing. Celery (**2**) is a perfect colour to balance dark green. In a traditional house use the darker colour below the dado rail and palest celery above.

4

5

Soft fern (**3**) is a great colour for the floor — either choose a good quality carpet or paint the floorboards.

Dark forest (**4**) can be used for the skirting-boards and window frames to create an outline. Pale mint (**5**) is a fun highlight for cushions.

Bloomsbury *style*

Charleston House in Suffolk is a historical landmark and a celebration of the talents of the artists and writers (Virginia Woolf was one) who lived there in the early 20th century. The house was painted in colours like emerald (**1**), now synonymous with the 1920s.

Colours inspired by the famous Bloomsbury set.

The main dark, yellowed green is brought to life when combined with these dusty, mid-tone colours. Let your imagination run wild with these hues and paint patterns on the doors, tabletops and even the floor.

Celadon green (**2**) is a great soft, neutral colour upon which to build the remaining colours. Use it for the floor.

Dusty rose (**3**) and Tuscan orange (**4**) can be used for patterned fabrics.

Olive (**5**) is a wonderfully rich green that is perfect for painting furniture.

Spring-fresh *floral*

Leafy green is a perfect background to petal shades.

Leaf (**1**) is a yellow-based, natural shade of green that takes reference from the garden. We should never overlook Mother Nature's use of colour as our primary source of inspiration. This palette can have a seasonal twist with more pale pink in summer and rich purple in winter.

1

2

3

Use the main leaf (**1**) green for the walls. In a small room this dark shade may seem a little oppressive, so mix with lily (**2**) on a single wall or on half walls split by a dado rail.

With such dark walls, you will need to use a paler shade for the floor and ceiling. The more adventurous designer could paint the floor in petal pink (**3**).

4

5

Lavender and purple (**4, 5**) are perfect for upholstery and curtains to bring some real colour into the room. If you want only a touch of purple then use this for the cushions and choose leaf-green furniture.

Pea and lime, *energetic and juicy*

This is not a palette for the faint-hearted. A zingy mix of refreshing greens is vigorous and powerful, bringing new life and lots of energy into an area. Pea (**1**), the main green, is fresh and strong and would work well in an area with lots of traffic, such as a hall or stairwell.

Revive a tired space in the home with invigorating brights.

Pampas grass (**2**) is a light, yellowed green that could be used for painting a wooden floor or for staining pale woods such as pine.

Sage (**3**) is a great colour for fabrics and upholstery. Choose heavy wovens to make a curtain across the front door to keep out the cold.

Lime (**4**) is a striking accent colour that is great for fun details. Choose transparent materials, such as glass or resins.

Forest (**5**) can be used for a rug and for picture frames to give a darker level and ground this vivid palette.

Muted, *quiet and tranquil*

A meditative mix of softened greens and cool, subdued blues.

Green has been said to have meditative qualities. These softened, greyed-off tones are perfect for a simple, composed atmosphere in any area of the home. Avocado (**1**) evokes an instant feeling of well-being for a bathroom, and it will induce a peaceful sleep in the bedroom.

Choose natural materials in this room. If possible source natural pigment-based paints, such as limewash or distemper. These paints are not only good for your home and the environment, they also have an unmistakable natural, flat quality.

Use cool blue and grey-blue (**2**, **3**) in a flat finish to wash wooden cupboards and panelling. If you have a wooden floor use these shades to stain it.

Spearmint (**5**) brings a fresh injection of colour perfect for fabrics, curtains, towels and bedcovers in crisp cotton.

Modern *graphic contrasts*

This is a playful collaboration of brights and darks. Opposing colours are placed next to each other for dramatic contrast. Green and red are opposites on the colour wheel, but can have a striking effect when used together, as seen here with lime (**1**), peacock (**4**) and burnt orange (**5**).

A contemporary mix of strong colours for a fun interior.

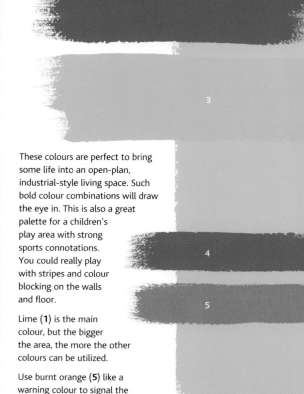

These colours are perfect to bring some life into an open-plan, industrial-style living space. Such bold colour combinations will draw the eye in. This is also a great palette for a children's play area with strong sports connotations. You could really play with stripes and colour blocking on the walls and floor.

Lime (**1**) is the main colour, but the bigger the area, the more the other colours can be utilized.

Use burnt orange (**5**) like a warning colour to signal the corners of the room or create arrows that lead the eye.

Chintz: *flowery and traditional*

A summer palette of floral colours for a feminine interior.

Red and green can work well together. Being opposite each other on the colour wheel, red really stands out from the main mint ice cream (**1**) colour so you may only need a small amount to make an impression. White is very important in this mix since it stops the colours from clashing.

The main green is rather strong, so antique ivory (**2**) and pink (**3**) can be used to balance the intensity. For a vintage approach use white-and-green striped wallpaper.

This room should focus around floral patterns that will mix all five colours. Cath Kidston produces some fantastic, modern fabrics in rose and flower patterns.

Lipstick red (**4**) is to be used sparingly – a single red glass for example.

Moss green (**5**) can be used for larger furniture to balance the prettiness of the room.

Romantic *ballet*

Degas painted ballet dancers rehearsing and while backstage. He used layers of delicate greens and pinks to create a light, diffused effect. Inspiration can be taken from these fragile layers of colour. Gooseberry (**1**) is perfect for a graceful bedroom or a light and airy living room or conservatory.

Soft colours inspired by the painter Degas.

1

2

3

The main gooseberry (**1**) is the strongest of all the colours here. Layer the four remaining colours slowly within the room, as if you are an artist creating a masterpiece.

Use palest fennel (**2**) for the ceiling and floor. Dusty plaster (**3**) is a perfect, neutral shade to use for large pieces of furniture, such as the sofa and armchairs.

4

5

Mix layers of organza in powder peach (**4**) and ballet pink (**5**) for an unusual window dressing. Also, use the pink for satin-covered cushions and hang a Degas print above the fireplace.

Open *garden*

Bring the outside in with garden-inspired, fresh, light colours.

Make the living space feel like it is a part of the garden by choosing leafy greens and pistachio (**1**), light and airy neutral shades and splashes of fuchsia. Rooms that open out onto a garden can be exaggerated by opening out the wall and replacing it with sliding glass doors.

With as much natural daylight as possible coming into the house, the main fresh green will come to life and transform tired walls. Use mid-green (**2**) for the furnishings: it is a good basic, versatile colour that can be changed with your moods from one season to another.

Pale-green tint (**3**) and concrete (**4**) can be used in an architectural way on beams and pillars. You could even continue the paving slabs from outside to inside.

Fuchsia (**5**) is a red-hot colour, great for any accessory, such as cushions, mirror frames or flowers.

Aromatic *pine and lavender*

A fresh colour like pine (**1**) not only delights the eye, but stirs the senses by invoking the wonderful scents of nature. Use tactile and textural surfaces, such as glossy plastics and fluffy mohair, to really bring the colours to life. Place sprigs of lavender on tabletops or in vases and fill the room with green, leafy plants.

A sensual palette of fresh colours that mimic nature.

This is a great bathroom palette with fresh tones of green, calming pales and invigorating lavender.

Choose rose tint (**2**) for the bathroom fixtures since this colour can be taken in almost any direction when you need to change the room.

Soft lavender (**3**) is a great colour for the woodwork, including the bath surround and bathroom cabinet.

Lavender (**4**) and pine (**5**) are strong colours so have fun with them. Visit charity shops for unusual china. Cover old books with wallpaper and leave them as gifts for your guests to unwrap.

Apples, *blossoms and sunlight*

Pale apple green brings us the colour of spring.

Using light apple (**1**) is a great way of bringing the outside in. Greens can really lift a room, and whether you're decorating a traditional cottage or a modern apartment, pale greens suit every style. Calming and easy on the eye, sweet apple tones offer a pretty alternative for any bedroom.

1

2

3

A look inspired by new spring buds and warm summer mornings. Complete it with natural, pale-wood furniture – and always have fresh flowers on show to complement the colours.

4

5

Imagine the sunlight filtering through the window and capture that perfect sunny yellow (**2**) to combine with spring green (**3**) for a warming and inviting mix.

For a truly garden-inspired touch, use delicate highlights of apple-blossom pink (**5**) or cherry blossom (**4**) for scatter cushions and rugs.

Sorbet, *lemon meringue and fig*

This wonderful, contemporary mix of light and bright shades is inspired by desserts. Lime sorbet (**1**) is a wonderfully refreshing colour. It will deepen as you apply the paint to the walls and change dramatically from day to night. All colours are given a yellowed hue in the evening with artificial light.

A mouth-watering palette of fruity colours.

Fig (**3**) is a great fabric colour. Use it on upholstery and either go for a more glamorous feel with shiny velvet or a rustic approach with a matt, woven fabric.

Strawberry mousse (**2**) can be used for the woodwork and to exaggerate original features, such as a ceiling rose or shutters.

Sour lime and green lemon (**4**, **5**) add a sharp injection of flavour in glassware; mix within prints for fabrics and bold ceramics. Serve delicate cakes and fluffy lemon meringue pies on brightly coloured serving dishes to really get the juices flowing.

Classic, *refined Georgian*

Refer to historical interiors for good taste and design.

Greens like sea foam (**1**) have been popular interior colours for centuries, however, some of the first green pigments were poisonous. Visit stately homes or restored historic houses for inspiration – most paint companies now produce a historic range.

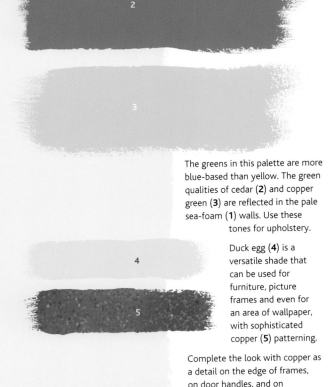

The greens in this palette are more blue-based than yellow. The green qualities of cedar (**2**) and copper green (**3**) are reflected in the pale sea-foam (**1**) walls. Use these tones for upholstery.

Duck egg (**4**) is a versatile shade that can be used for furniture, picture frames and even for an area of wallpaper, with sophisticated copper (**5**) patterning.

Complete the look with copper as a detail on the edge of frames, on door handles, and on candleholders and cushions.

Refreshing, *verdant, dewy*

Pale aqua (**1**) is clear and uplifting. Subtle colours can have an intense effect on a room and this green will reflect maximum light. Mix with contrasting shades of dark, bright and light colours for a graphic edge in a strictly modern yet soothing and meditative environment.

An invigorating choice of colours to lift the spirits.

Use bright white (**2**) to further lift the light levels of this room. If you have a small bathroom with little natural light, this colour scheme is perfect. Use strong recessed spot lighting and place tiny bulbs around the mirror for a glamorous touch.

Deep, inky blue (**3**) is a wonderfully rich, luscious colour. Use this on the window and door frames. Use for ceramic bowls, soaps and miscellaneous objects.

Spearmint (**4**) and bright aqua (**5**) can be used in tinted glass shelving and coloured glass jars. Source bright, fluffy aqua towels for a touch of fun.

Peppermint, *chocolate and coffee*

A sugar-rush of colour for a sweet, lively interior.

Peppermint (**1**) with chocolate brown is an age-old interior combination. This palette is rich and comfortable but with a tantalizing twist. The greens stimulate while the browns soothe and relax the soul. Use these colours in a living room for a stunning finish.

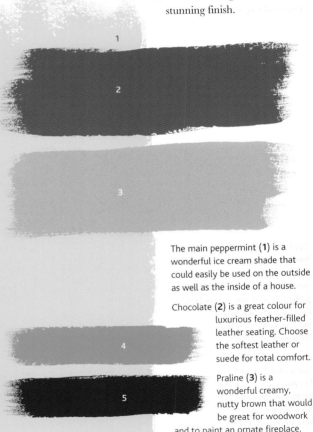

The main peppermint (**1**) is a wonderful ice cream shade that could easily be used on the outside as well as the inside of a house.

Chocolate (**2**) is a great colour for luxurious feather-filled leather seating. Choose the softest leather or suede for total comfort.

Praline (**3**) is a wonderful creamy, nutty brown that would be great for woodwork and to paint an ornate fireplace.

Roast coffee (**5**) is for the dark-wood furniture — keep shapes modern and simple.

Use mint leaf (**4**) for details, such as cushions, rugs and glassware.

Urban *cityscape*

It is not only the natural landscape that can inspire an artist or designer. Modern cityscapes are bursting with colour and design inspiration too. Cool grey and architectural green (**1**) together with traffic-signal brights make for a fantastic interior colour scheme for a contemporary space.

Take a moment to look at the world and be inspired.

Bring external features into the home, such as polished concrete (**3**) pillars or flooring, or use sign graphics as quirky wall decorations.

Signal green (**2**) is a great colour to use on a single wall or even an area of flooring in an open-plan space.

Signal red (**4**) can be utilized in many ways. Try painting stripes across the floor. Make a feature of a single piece of furniture such as a designer chair or a modern, coloured, resin-coated set of drawers or sleek china cabinet.

Khaki (**5**), a great basic, can be used for the remaining furniture.

Mint, *citrus and ocean greens*

Use spearmint freshness to wake the senses.

Refreshing mint (**1**) creates a sublime yet invigorating wake-me-up bathroom palette. Light and rejuvenating blue greens have been proven to lift the spirit and clear the mind, giving a perfect start to the day.

1

2

3

4

5

Ideal for a modern bathroom or shower room, these shades need to be kept pure and distinct in order to make a real impact.

Use these lively colours with chrome fittings and crisp white furniture for a fresh and contemporary feel.

Citrus lime greens (**2**, **3**) are used as the main accent colours for the woodwork.

Choose rich, deep-ocean greens (**4**, **5**) for glassware and graphic images for the walls.

Uplifting *and natural*

This fabulous pale jade (**1**) is contrasted with natural straw
colours and a bright sunshine yellow. By complementing the
bright tones with natural yellowed neutrals, an easy palette that
would work well in a kitchen or family room is formed.
Lots of daylight from large windows will
help enhance the colours.

*Mix bright and
natural shades for
energetic rooms.*

1

2

3

4

5

Use jade (**1**) for the kitchen
cabinets for the look of a fun
1950s-style diner.

Sunshine yellow (**2**) is often used
in kitchens, but always opt for a
more 'orangey' yellow
for instant warmth. Use
this colour on one or all
of the walls, depending
on how much you like
a wake-up call in
the morning.

Avocado (**3**) and
string (**4**) are perfect for natural
surfaces in the room, such as sisal
or coir matting for the floor and
basketry for storage.

Seal brown (**5**) is a warm tone that
could work for upholstery, door
handles and picture frames.

Saturated, *surreal and bold*

Strong colours make a bold, hyper-real statement.

Sea green (**1**) is a strong, bright green. This tone could either be mixed with softer shades for a pretty, ice-cream-sundae palette or with rich colours for an adventurous colour scheme, which will have dramatic effects in any space. Make sure you keep these daring colours in balance.

True blue (**2**) can be used for the soft furnishings. Choose modern furniture shapes that are blocky and square, rather than traditional, rounded furniture. Fabrics should be plain and simple – let the colours do all the work.

Powder blue (**3**) can be used on the woodwork.

Mauve and deep purple (**4**, **5**) can be used for accessories and quirky details. Paint some unusual ornaments, such as a cast bust or a garden gnome, for weird but wonderful accessories.

Exotic *antique green*

These flat, mid-tone colours look like they have existed for many years. Soft and almost faded, verdigris (**1**), pink and neutrals conjure up many historical references. Wash the walls and use a flat finish to give the colours an aged look. Source antique, hand-printed fabrics to cover the bed or sofa.

Vintage colours from Africa and the Far East.

Softened pink and cashmere (**2, 3**) are great colours for patterned fabrics, such as embroidered or hand-printed fabrics, to cover the bed or sofa.

Forest floor (**4**) can be used for natural woven floor matting or dark stained floorboards. Paint simple wooden furniture in the same colour.

Use recycled green glass (**5**) for accessories, such as heavy tumblers for drinks and tea lights. Hang green glass beads in the door or at the window for a real bazaar feeling.

Enamel, *green glass and glaze*

Rich, modern greens range from softened lichen to peacock.

Green has more variations than any other colour, so the possibilities and combinations for a green room are endless. With such versatility the end result can be rustic simplicity or jewelled opulence. Mix sage (**1**) in matt and shiny surfaces with enamelled tiles and flat woodwork.

This is a great palette for a stylish and contemporary kitchen. Mix the new with the old by sourcing rustic green enamel earthenware pots and making a rich-green range the focus of the room.

Sage (**1**) and muted lichen (**2**) are the softest colours in the room and should be utilized the most.

In a kitchen use bright malachite (**3**) for tile or glass work surfaces and also for the tabletop.

Green tea (**4**) and peacock (**5**) are perfect for kitchen utensils, pots and glassware.

Ocean *green*

This ocean (**1**) colour is very versatile. Such a shade of green could be used in a bathroom, living area or kitchen with enormous success. There are a million different ocean colours and all change with the light levels. These wonderful blue-green tones are restorative and restful.

An exciting palette of sea greens with warm reds.

Use sea foam (**3**) for the flooring. In a bathroom go for painted wooden floorboards or paint squares of plywood in different levels of green to make a chequerboard pattern.

Use shell pink (**2**) for fluffy towels and rose-coloured soaps. In a living area, stripe this colour with sea foam for chair covers.

Buoy red (**5**) is the accent colour in the room. Use for stunning glassware or a splendid feature chandelier.

Deep ocean (**4**) can be used for the outline, the window frame, skirting-boards and dado rails.

Invigorating *turquoise*

Classic colours get a twist when combined with turquoise.

Bright colours do not always have to be matched with other brights. Here, softened grey greens and midnight blues take the sharp edge off the main turquoise (**1**). This palette would make a striking statement in a dining or living room.

For a really clever approach to design, mix the unexpected together. Lightest pink (**2**) is a perfect colour for upholstery. It's warm and cosy but still maintains an air of neutrality. Choose soft fabrics such as chenille, wool-mohair blends and imitation suede.

Grey-green (**3**) can be used for the carpet. It could also be used on one or several of the walls if the turquoise is too much.

Bottle green and deep midnight blue (**4, 5**) give the room some depth. Use these colours for mirror frames, table settings, candlesticks and lampshades.

Sun-parched *summer meadow*

This is a rather old-fashioned group of colours. Malachite (**1**) is reminiscent of gentlemen's smoking rooms or card tables. We have mixed this stronger green with a group of softened, nostalgic shades – the kind of colours you see after a long, dry period has scorched the grasses and dried up the earth.

A subtle collection of sentimental colours faded by the sun.

Pea pod (**2**) is a pretty green that would work well for curtains and fabrics.

Sun-bleached green (**3**) can be used for woodwork, doors, window shutters and shelving.

In a kitchen, faded terracotta (**5**) floor tiles and work surfaces would look fantastic. Fill old terracotta plant pots with meadow flowers, such as daisies, poppies and sweet peas.

Shell (**4**) can be used for the kitchen cabinets and for upholstery. Mix with the other accent colours in pretty floral patterns or soft tartan checks.

Blues

Indigo: *ancient mineral*

Deep, darkest indigo is one of the oldest dyes in the world.

With its roots in the Far East, the colour indigo (**1**) has always had exotic connotations. An ultramarine blue was used by the architect Louis Majorelle to decorate his home in Marrakesh. That blue is now an intrinsic part of modern architecture in Morocco.

Use deepest midnight blue (**4**) for upholstery and leather surfaces in the room. Try to use as many natural materials as possible and keep the paint flat. Mix with deep, natural pigment colours such as lapis lazuli (**3**) and red earth (**2**).

Rich gold (**5**) is the perfect colour to combine with solid and dark blues. Use it in a gloss or metallic finish on picture frames, mirror edges and even on skirting-boards or ornate crown moulding for a truly decadent atmosphere. Source place mats and candlesticks in gold leaf for the dining table.

Intense, *elegant and refined*

An intense Prussian blue (**1**) still looks fresh when combined with these soft tones. Rich, dark turquoise is contrasted with palest blue-greys and a shocking, raspberry highlight. For a kitchen, choose antique French-style cupboards and paint them in washes of the pale colours.

A striking play with dark and light needs a precise design.

Source pale blue-grey (**3**) stone for the floor, or use concrete as a contemporary flooring. Leave it unpolished for a more rustic look.

Cornflower (**2**) can be used for ceramics and storage jars stacked on the shelves.

Use rich raspberry (**5**) for soft furnishings and fabrics within the room. Choose either plain, woven fabrics for seat covers or stripes of the raspberry and grey (**4**).

Progressive, *modern and fresh*

Clashing colours can succeed if the balance is right.

Be daring in your colour choice and create a new dimension in the home. Bright turquoise (**1**) could be a cold colour to use in interior design. Mix cool shades with warmer accents to create a pleasing mood. Fresh, citrus shades complement and contrast with the turquoise.

This colour scheme is perfect for a modern, loft-style apartment, but could be just as interesting if used in a traditional interior.

Palest aqua tint (**2**) can be used for the woodwork since the main turquoise shade needs some pale tones to balance it out.

Light citrus (**3**) and wasabi (**4**) are to be mixed for the upholstery. Use either fine stripes of the two colours or, for the dining table, choose alternating colours for the chairs.

Peach (**5**) helps to warm up the palette. Use in geometric prints for cushions and curtains.

Weathered *beach huts*

This wonderful, deep-sky blue (**1**) is a happy and friendly colour to use in the home, great for a bathroom, kitchen or even a fun family living room. This palette can be made as kitsch as you like. Source flags to make into cushion covers and 1950s seaside postcards to frame on the wall.

A classic palette of colours inspired by sea front houses.

Search out quirky accessories such as nautical memorabilia like sailors' hats and use boating rope for curtain tiebacks, light pulls and towel rails.

This is all about the mix. Stripes of the main blue, white (**2**) and sand (**3**) can be painted on the wall or onto wood panelling for a real boating experience.

Winter sea (**5**) can be used for the flooring.

Use bright red (**4**) for plastic or enamel cups and plates. Make them a feature by hanging them from hooks along the wall.

Soft, *safe hideaway*

These dusty shades are restful and contemplative.

This palette is subdued and softened. Slate (**1**) is a dusky colour and easy on the eye. Such a palette is great for an office or quiet living area. Cocoon yourself in matt finishes that soak up exterior noises and create a peaceful haven away from the hustle and bustle of the world.

1

2

3

4

5

Use a thick, soft carpet in slate (**2**) for total comfort underfoot. Cover seating in brushed mohair, suede or cotton velour in seal grey (**3**) for a blurred finish to this cool, neutral shade.

Dusty pink (**4**) and foxglove (**5**) can be used to add feminine details and prevent it from becoming a vision of grey. These warm shades, while not overly pretty, help to create a touch of comfort within the room. Use the pinks sparingly on cushions and placed items around the room, such as a single vase or covered books.

Classic, *tailor-made comfort*

Mix soft woad blue (**1**) with warm and cosy terracottas and deep plum for a bold yet comfortable living room or kitchen. Blues look great with rich brown and earth tones. This combination could easily be used for a country-style or traditional Mediterranean kitchen, or a modern, bold living room.

Bring blues into a warm and inviting environment.

Use heavy, oversized furniture to match the heavy colours. Use plum (**5**) for leather chairs and luxury seat covers.

Pottery (**2**) and blue clay (**4**) are warm and inviting colours that should fit any room like a glove.

Terracotta (**3**) flooring has become very chic when used in modern kitchens and living areas. Source handmade tiles from Spain, France or Morocco for an instantly lived-in look. These tiles can be used for the floor, work surfaces, behind the sink and even on tabletops.

Bright, *inspiring, and lively*

Clean colours work well in a simple, stylized bathroom.

Bright aqua (**1**) is great for a bathroom. Use the yellow accent colours for ceramic or glass tiles on a strict, graphic, practical surface. Keep the look modern and simple since the bright colours need little decoration, and invest in quality chrome taps and details.

1

2

3

Lemon foam (**3**) can be used for any woodwork in the room. Keep the lines straight and smooth, and with a glossy finish.

Buttercup (**2**) can be used for the floor for a golden glow in the mornings. Choose this colour for a neon-tinted-glass shower cubicle.

4

5

Keep the bathroom simple in plain white (**4**), but look for modern designs and shapes such as a Marc Newson toilet, bath and sink.

Dark turquoise (**5**) is for the details. Have your favourite quote printed in vinyl lettering and run it around the walls for a quirky twist.

Delicate, *translucent twilight*

The clear and dainty tones of blue topaz (**1**) are like transparent coloured glass, and can be used in a light, airy bedroom or bathroom. Choose translucent, floaty fabrics for the windows and tinted glass for any lamps, candleholders or even a chandelier. Layer colours in clever patterns and shades to create depth within the room.

Dreamy, glassy tints for a sanctuary at home.

This room is characterized by underplayed luxury. Nothing in here is ostentatious, but every surface suggests pure indulgence.

Choose celeriac (**2**) and sage (**3**) for chalky, flat painted surfaces around the room.

Slate blue (**4**) is perfect for upholstery in soft and tactile fabrics.

Choose lavender (**5**) for the few precious details that are on show in this room, such as heavy glass vases and oversized bowls filled with floating candles. Everything else should be cleverly hidden out of view.

Porcelain, *velvet and patterns*

This palette is inspired by vintage drawing rooms.

Forget-me-not (**1**) would be great in a period house with lots of original features. In a living room or dining area a vintage-inspired wallpaper could be used on a single wall for a touch of decadent nostalgia. Choose a hand-blocked paper if possible for a truly original look.

The wonderful greens (**2**, **3**) can be used as much or as little in this room as you desire. Carpets, curtains and upholstery can all be in these tones. Either choose plain woven fabrics, felted wool or low-sheen velvet. Opt for sofa-style armchairs with buttoned backs.

These colours will look equally dramatic whether in full daylight or in sultry candlelight. The levels of peach (**4**, **5**) bring a touch of light into this room. These colours are great as accents within patterning for wallpaper or decorative cushions. Choose pale peach ceramics and source peach-tinted glass light fittings.

Streamlined *retro kitchenette*

Seawater (**1**) works well as a neutral backdrop. Here we have chosen classic beige and tobacco; these traditional 1940s interior shades are once more at the forefront of home decorating styles. Choose furniture shapes reminiscent of the 1940s and 50s, and accessorize with bold, geometric patterned fabrics and prints.

Mix modern with retro finds for an individual design.

Use this palette in a dining area or open-plan kitchen. Go for retro styling, such as a breakfast or cocktail bar in tobacco (**2**) with high stools in beige (**3**) and sliding-glass cupboard doors. Many interior companies are now making excellent reproductions of classic styles from this era.

Accessorize with cocktail glasses and a retro-style fridge, toaster and kettle in milkshake (**4**).

Source retro food packaging from the 40s and 50s in teal (**5**) and stack on shelves or countertops for a quirky touch.

Modern pattern, *graphic flowers*

A contemporary use of florals takes blues to the next level.

Aquamarine (**1**) is a lovely background shade – it gives a clean, bright finish without being overpowering. Today there are many fabric and wallpaper designers using patterning and floral imagery in a modern, graphic way. Look for styles of wallpaper that will inspire fresh palettes.

1

2

3

Use pale pistachio (**2**) for the woodwork. To make this space less feminine keep details to a minimum and lines clean.

Fresh mint (**3**) can be used in pattern with bubble gum (**4**) and fresh aniseed (**5**). You may need to include white in this room too, as a background in some of the prints, to break up the use of colour.

4

5

Bold, patterned upholstery is currently very popular, however, if you do not want to invest in pattern for all of the upholstery, then opt for plain aniseed. Accessorize with patterned cushions and curtains, and even patterned plates and cups.

Soothingly *neutral*

Sky blue (**1**) is brought down to a relaxing, tranquil environment with these tinted greys and warm neutrals. Create a completely serene atmosphere with underpowering shades. Nothing in this room should stand out too much; everything is easy on the eye and everything has a place or a purpose.

An easy, tranquil mix of cool and warm hues.

1

2

3

Morning mist (**2**) is a wonderfully light and translucent colour that would work well on both matt and glossy surfaces. Use this colour for the woodwork.

Dove (**3**) can be used for soft furnishings. In a bedroom layer textures and textiles for a cosy night's sleep.

4

Warm neutrals (**4**, **5**) add a touch of luxury to the room. Choose suede for seat covers and soft sheepskin rugs for the floor. Source natural, carved blond-coloured wood for bowls and candlesticks.

5

Chalky, *dusted powder*

Pale aqua is subdued with whitened shades of grey.

This palette utilizing pale cyan (**1**) is inspired by the horizon at dawn. At this time of day colours are not overpowering – all are muted and each colour blends happily into the next. That is how this room should seem: all colours are flat and easy on the eye creating a smooth transition from floor to ceiling.

1

2

3

Milky pink (**2**) is the colour of yogurt; rich berry colours are flattened with the addition of dairy to create a softened tone. Use this colour for soft furnishings in the room. Opt for felted- wool fabrics that reflect rather than absorb light to intensify the whitening effect.

4

5

Two levels of washed stone (**3**, **4**) are perfect for the woodwork and flooring. Again, opt for matt surfaces such as carpet or washed wood.

Raspberry bloom (**5**) is the strongest colour so use it for curtains and accessories.

Whisper light, *feather*

Lightness is key to many things in modern design: not simply with regards to colour and weight, but also the uplifting, almost spiritual qualities that lightness provides. A light, airy room in ice blue (**1**) can change your mood and instantly make you feel less stressed and more at ease.

Pale colours are a breath of fresh air in a dark, tired room.

1

2

3

Delicate shades like these can create a wonderfully relaxing and soothing environment. Many of us are wary of blue in the home since it can create a cold atmosphere. However, blue is said to provoke clear thinking and relieve the effects of insomnia, so use it in a study or bedroom.

4

Super-pale lemon (**2**) and pearl (**3**) can be used to paint the ceiling and the floor to exaggerate the expanse of space in a room.

5

The strongest shades of blue (**4, 5**) can be used for woodwork, fresh linen on the bed and upholstery.

Provençal *lavender blue*

Colours inspired by country homes in France.

Blue is one of the most international of all shades. Many countries favour blue in their traditional housing and architecture. This palette of Provençal lavender blue (**1**) and soft pink is inspired by the country houses of Provence, with plaster walls and blue doors and window frames.

1

2

3

The main lavender blue can be used for the flooring and the ceiling since white is too harsh against these softened colours.

Soft pink (**2**) is the wall colour. Try to find a natural, water- or lime-based paint for a rustic, matt finish. You could even mix the paint with a wash to create an aged finish on the walls.

4

5

French blue (**3**) is for the woodwork and door. Use the darker shade of ink (**5**) for painting kitchen cupboards.

Slate (**4**) can be used for heavy work surfaces and also for neutral furnishings.

Distinctive *and distinguished*

This cool blue (**1**) palette could either be used in a traditional setting for a living or dining area, or in a more modern, graphic way for a funky kitchen or den. The levels of light and dark can be used to create spaces within the room. If you have dark furniture then place it in front of a pale wall for maximum effect.

Individual colours that can be used to suit your taste.

1

2

3

The levels of green in this room are more yellow based, and bring warmth and light to the main cool blue (**1**). Greens and blues are a classic combination that can easily be used in a modern setting.

Soft avocado (**2, 3**) colours are great for a kitchen. Use in tones on bevelled kitchen doors – the darker shade creates a shadow.

4

5

Emerald (**4**) can be used for a striking tiled floor. Go for a resin-based glossy finish for a stunning, jewel-like effect.

Black (**5**) can be used in Japanese-style serving plates and bowls and polished granite work surfaces.

Country-*cabin chic*

A romantic palette of rustic browns and fresh blues.

This powder blue (**1**) palette is inspired by the wooden cabins of Scandinavia and Canada, old-fashioned homes that are becoming sought-after cottages for city dwellers. Exposed wood and brick, hand-carved furniture and traditional woven fabrics create a safe haven from modern life.

1

2

3

Powder blue (**1**) can be used for the flooring or to paint furniture. As much of this environment will be rich browns and natural wood surfaces, the blue acts as a fresh and contrasting colour.

Use soft putty (**2, 3**) colours to wash natural wood furniture.

4

5

This wonderful natural blue (**5**) would have been used in traditional woven fabrics and mixed with white. Source the traditional fabrics of the area for bedspreads, tablecloths and blankets.

Baby blue, *baby pink*

When decorating a room for children, baby blue (**1**) is traditionally used for a boy and pink for a girl. Today, the barriers are not so strict and you can mix the colours as you wish. Here we have a balanced mix of blues and pinks and lights and darks, which could be used for a child's or grown-up's bedroom.

A naive palette of colours that is not just for children.

Use soft dove grey (**2**) for the floor and woodwork. A grey shade in the mix will prevent the room from becoming too sickly. Use grey in patterns within the room for cushions or bedspreads.

Stripes or checks in baby pink (**3**) and dove grey can be used to make loose covers for chairs and cushions.

Use raspberry cordial (**5**) and tutti-frutti (**4**) for fun details around the room. Why not hang a hammock instead of using conventional seating? Have several light fixtures put in the ceiling and hang different shaped shades from them.

Wedgwood *and delftware details*

A palette inspired by 17th-century European ceramics.

A palette of china blue (**1**) is inspired by classic Wedgwood and delftware ceramics from England and Holland. The blue-and-white motifs of both designs are famous around the world. Advancements in the production of blues and greens in the 17th century made them favoured interior colours of the era.

1

2

3

Originally invented by the Chinese and then copied by the Europeans, the blue glazes and patterns of Wedgwood and delftware have inspired design ever since. For a traditional look you could paint some of the naive scenes from the ceramics onto a wall. Alternatively, many DIY shops sell great imitation delft tiles that look fantastic in the kitchen, around the fireplace or in the bathroom.

4

5

Use a darker blue (**3**) to pick out features in a room.

The green levels (**4**, **5**) can be used for furnishing and carpets throughout the ground floor.

Violet, *pansy and blueberry*

Intense violet blues can be so strong that they look artificial even in nature, for example on certain pansies. Blues that occur in nature are a wonderful inspiration for the home. This shade of blueberry (**1**) has definite red undertones, which make it an easy, warm colour to live with.

Warm, violet colours encourage soft decorating in blue.

1

2

3

A symphony of gorgeous blue-violets (**1**, **3**, **4**) are played off against each other. These tones can be used to highlight the architectural details in a room.

Use white (**2**) for the ceiling to lighten the mood. If you want a traditional dado rail, try striping white and blue-violet below the rail.

4

Blushing pink (**5**) is a great counter colour to the cooler, violet shades. This injection of pink enhances the warmer quality of the blues and rounds off the mix. If you take away the pink, the palette becomes a single blur of shades of blue.

5

Regal *blue*

Take inspiration from the paintings of the old masters.

Historically, blues such as cornflower (**1**) were often used to represent royalty or religious figures. Ultramarine was made from a mineral called lapis lazuli, and it was more expensive than gold. The luxury and rarity of this colour propelled it into the realms of wealth.

Combinations of blue, cream and brown are classic and can instantly create a luxurious environment. Use this palette for an aristocratic living room or library in the home.

Royal blue (**2**) can be used to paint the ceiling. For a very grand finish paint tiny stars or have miniature bulbs set to create your very own constellation.

Use cream (**3**) for expensive leather seating and deep-pile plush carpeting.

Noisette and walnut (**4**, **5**) are perfect for the fireplace, small tables, heavy picture frames and leather-bound books.

Spiritual, *mysterious blue*

Blue, the colour of the ocean and the sky on sunny days, always lifts the spirits and recharges your batteries. It represents space and freedom, it is soothing and relaxing. All colours change the mood of a room, but blues such as hyacinth (**1**) can take you on any spiritual journey you desire.

A blue palette reflects a search for enlightenment.

Blues and greens, the colours of the natural landscape, always work well in interiors. Levels of light and dark will create a cocooned atmosphere. Darker colours help to keep out noise.

Spirit green (**2**) is a great colour for window frames. Using green around the window helps to bring nature indoors.

Deep forest greens (**3**, **4**) can be used for the flooring and curtains. Choose low-level seating and rugs to lounge on.

Use ultramarine (**5**) for silk cushions, incense burners and blue glass lighting.

Casual *denim blue*

Get inspired by your wardrobe: use denim fabrics and fashion.

Denim (**1**) is no longer the reserve of students and cowboys, it is now seen as a quality fabric, used in luxury design for interiors as well as fashion. The hard-wearing quality of denim makes it a brilliant interior design solution. Choose from darkest indigo to pale stonewashed varieties.

Denim (**1**) is a flat colour that needs lots of natural daylight and good accents to lift it.

Use dark denim (**2**) for seat covers in the kitchen, bathroom or den. For a funky dining area, cover chair seats with the fabric and use denim for napkins too.

Stonewashed (**3**) can be used for the wood-work. This lighter shade of denim will help to marry all the colours in the scheme.

The mauve shades (**4**, **5**) will give warmth to the room. For a fun twist use old T-shirts for cushion covers and lampshades.

Playful, *mischievous mix*

A clashing palette of bright bluebell (**1**) and reds will create a lively environment – colours do not always have to be in harmony in order to work. Primary colours such as blue and red always make a strong statement in an interior. Here we use levels of light and dark colours to play tricks on the eye.

A fun mix of blues and reds for a funky bedroom interior.

Use large-scale graphic imagery on the bedcovers. You can even get personal photographs printed onto fabrics.

Use blueberry (**3**) for the carpet or flooring. Choose a flat material such as linoleum or rubber tiles.

Ink (**2**) can be used for the woodwork and to paint fine pinstripes on the walls in gloss paint.

Candy pink (**4**) and rouge (**5**) should be used in patterning or to paint details such as door handles and picture frames.

Bejewelled: *sapphire, emerald*

A precious palette of glossy surfaces and sparkling details.

Sapphire (**1**) is a rich, dazzling colour that is intensified in gloss and metallic surfaces. In a dining or living area, paint a lacquer or varnish over the wall colour to produce a gloss finish. This will reflect light into the room and saturate the colours further. Reinvent old furniture with glossy coats.

For decadent details use jewellery to adorn the walls. Collect costume jewellery from a charity shop and pin brooches and necklaces to the wall in shapes and patterns.

Jet (**2**) can be used for the woodwork. Also use it for the tabletops or work surfaces. If you sand each coat of gloss paint and apply it carefully, a truly glassy finish can be achieved.

Emerald and jade (**4**, **5**) can be used for glass light shades. Mix emerald with a metallic binder to paint mirror frames and the fireplace surround.

Rustic *farmhouse*

Rich dark blues have worked well with faded country stone reds and have been used all over Europe for centuries. This palette using French navy (**1**) takes inspiration from these simple yet effective colour combinations for a great kitchen or any room that opens out onto a garden.

Country colours for interiors and exteriors.

Dark blue (**2**) is a richer shade of the French navy (**1**). Use this for the woodwork inside and out.

Find blue ceramic planters and dark wood (**3**) boxes to fill with dark-leaved foliage such as cordyline.

Use bark chippings around the plants to discourage weeds from growing too quickly, and to give a constant hint of colouration.

Continue the theme from outside to indoors with red flagstone (**5**) floors and lots of surfaces in pale terracotta (**4**).

Mediterranean *island*

Inspired by white-washed houses and hot summer nights.

You may be inspired by the colours you find on your travels, but while rich, Mediterranean blue (**1**) and warm peaches look great in a sunny coastal village, they may not have the same effect in your home. Test colours on the walls before committing to a shade.

1

2

3

Traditionally the villages of southern Spain, Greece, Italy and France are painted lime white to reflect the heat of the sun. Here we have chosen a warmer cream (**2**) that will be more cosy in an interior environment.

Hazy sky (**3**) can be used for the floorboards and window frames. Also use it to paint mirrors or picture frames and any cupboards.

4

5

Peach and sunset orange (**4**, **5**) are hot, balmy colours that can be used in stripes or checks with the cream for fabrics. Choose hand-painted ceramics and bowls full of exotic fruits to finish the room.

Open *space*

Use paler colours for worktops in a kitchen to reflect the light. Rich ink (**1**) is lifted by a medley of paler tones. Deepest blue colours are deceiving in that they do not make the room appear smaller, but tend to open out a space and offer more light.

A simple blue-and-white palette gives a room a fresh feeling.

Choose scrubbed floorboards and simple wooden shutters at the window painted in buff (**2**). Why not hand paint folk-style patterns around the edge of doors and chairs? Leave woodwork clean and scrubbed.

For a more traditional look choose checked or polka-dot fabrics in pale grey (**3**) and air-force blue (**5**) for the seat covers, curtains, and napkins.

Details in here can be kept basic with an old-fashioned butler's sink and white or pale grey ceramics and crockery.

Violets

Blackberry, *cranberry and violet*

Blackberry violet is enlivened by flashes of cranberry.

Blackberry (**1**) is almost colourless, so it needs to be combined with some ambitious highlights to make the room inviting. Use this palette in a living or dining area for sumptuous relaxation. Tinted greys accentuate period features in a room, such as a grand fireplace, cornices or window shutters.

Storm-cloud grey (**2**) and violet-grey (**3**) furniture can be inspired by the 1930s, with elongated, low chairs and even a deep-cranberry (**4**) chaise longue.

Choose velvets and satins in cranberry and peony (**5**) to give depth to these colours. Make sure the pale grey carpet is top quality and the curtains cascade to the floor. For a modern twist have cranberry-dyed sheepskins sewn together to create a huge rug.

Keep flowers in the room to stop the greys from being overbearing. Choose pink lilies for dramatic contrast with the violet walls.

Magical *and theatrical*

Dark grape (**1**) is one of the most sumptuous and decadent colours available in paints today. This rich colour has an aromatic quality, evoking images of ancient opium dens, lavish palaces and theatrical settings with over-the-top curtains and meticulous decoration.

A medley of violets for a decadent, decorated room.

Purple is not a colour for everyone, however, when mixed with these dusty lavenders and chocolates, it is instantly irresistible.

Use the softened, dusky tones of dusty lavenders (**2**, **3**) for the woodwork, including armoires or chests of drawers in the bedroom.

Purple haze (**4**), the brightest of the colours, can be used for satin scatter cushions on the bed. Search for purple glass drawer handles, cocktail glasses or candlesticks.

Use bitter fig (**5**) for luxurious, satin quilted bedcovers.

Crocus, *lavender and lichen*

A luscious palette of rich, natural shades and floral tints.

Imperial purple (**1**) needs light colours to lift it, such as pale crocus (**3**) and soft iris (**2**). This palette can be altered to suit your personal preferences. If dark colours seem oppressive or the room you are working in is not very big, use pale crocus on one or two of the walls.

A completely purple room would be too much for most of us, so use a colour like lichen (**4**) for the floor to lighten the mood.

Upholstery colours change depending on how many walls you choose to paint dark or light. In front of the pale crocus, choose bark (**5**), and in front of the dark purple choose pale crocus.

Soft iris (**2**) can be used for accessories such as lamp-shades, cushions and elaborate tassels to tie back the curtains, and for the tiles around the fireplace.

Garden *fresh*

Greens are often seen as a neutral shade since they complement all of the primary colours. Here, we see just how good violets, like iris (**1**), and greens can look together. A combination taken straight from the garden is lightened and lifted into a pretty yet modern bedroom or bathroom.

Violets and greens always complement each other.

Clear watery greens (**2**, **3**) are wonderfully light and refreshing colours that will lift the iris (**1**) shade. Use for glossy woodwork and bathroom fixtures. Bring lots of light into the room with multiple mirrors or a simple wall of mirrored glass above the bath.

Use dusty mauve (**5**) for the matt flooring.

Blue ripple (**4**) can be used for glassware in the bathroom or for candleholders for a relaxing bathtime. Use lavender oil and fresh cedar to complement the use of natural garden shades.

Storm-cloud violet, *new dawn*

Warmed, neutral shades sit happily on a mauve backdrop.

Yellow sits opposite purple on the colour wheel. The cool and warm characteristics of the two shades complement each other and have become a classic mix in modern interior design. Storm cloud (**1**) takes inspiration from an overcast sky, with a streak of sunshine breaking through.

The main background colour creates a perfect outline around pale straw and sunset colours. Choose matt linen in light straw (**3**) for the soft furnishings.

Sandstone (**2**) is a good colour for stone, carpet or natural woven matting, such as seagrass or sisal.

Pink cloud (**4**) can be used for curtains and seat covers.

Use sunset orange (**5**) carefully and selectively with a couple of cushions placed on the sofa and a round vase of autumn roses on the mantle.

Opulent *and dramatic*

In the 1920s, after World War I, purple became a symbol of freedom. After years of grief and tension, wearing purple and using it in the home in colours like amethyst (**1**) seemed like a very extravagant thing to do. The colour became synonymous with the flappers who danced all night and lived outrageously.

Jewel tones give a decadent, decorated feel to a room.

This rich yet lively group of colours will create real drama in any room in the house. The amethyst (**1**) walls need good lighting to lift them. Use this palette for a sexy, indulgent bathroom or for a theatrical dining room where the guests become the actors and the food is colour coordinated.

Deep midnight (**2**) can be used for bathroom fixtures or dining furniture with a high-gloss finish.

Use bright, bold shades of turquoise (**4**, **5**) for glassware, and use candles and low lighting to bring the glass to life and allow it to sparkle around the room.

Scented *lavender*

An aromatic palette of garden blossoms in full bloom.

Cool lavender (**1**) and strong floral colours evoke images of romantic, hot summer evenings. This room should ideally open out onto a rose garden, but if you are not blessed with such a thing, then simply fill the window boxes with miniature roses and pungent lavender.

Imagine falling asleep with the soft scent of the garden floating in through the open window. Here, we capture that moment in colour, and make it last through the winter months.

These pretty colours will lift the spirits on dark mornings. Use the pistachio (**2**) for translucent layers at the window and for a glass chandelier.

Antique green (**3**) can be used for the woodwork, crown moulding and built-in cupboards. Have lots of mirrors in here, too, to bring in maximum light.

Rose pink (**4**) and scented stock (**5**) can be used to embroider linen.

Smart, *stylish and classy*

This group of colours could decorate a luxurious living room or dining area. Mauve (**1**) is a wonderfully decadent shade within which to dine. This colour will change dramatically with different lighting, offering a light, fresh lunch room and a rich and opulent evening space.

Violet colours work well in formal settings.

Choose fabrics, textures and surfaces carefully because quality is everything. Pale woods, such as pine and ash, can look expensive in the right setting. Use natural leather and suede tones (**2**, **3**) for napkins and place mats.

Silver always works well with violet shades, so invest in some silver napkin rings and picture frames.

Regal purple (**4**) looks fantastic on deep-pile velvets for the curtains and dining-chair seats. Choose a patterned or textured velvet to exaggerate the depth of colour.

Cool, *masculine loft living*

An urban palette for modern, open-plan bachelor lofts.

This quirky palette using violet-grey (**1**) could bring life into a large space lacking focus. By using architectural details, such as pillars and joists, as features and sharp, acid flashes of colour around the room, you can turn an empty shell into a modern, sophisticated environment.

Violet-grey (**1**) and storm-cloud grey (**4**) can be used to tint or paint the concrete surfaces in the space. Polished concrete is fast becoming a material of choice in many modern homes.

Pale aqua (**2**) is used to paint the remaining wall space in the area, encouraging calmness and tranquillity.

Peacock (**3**) and glowing orange (**5**) can be used to draw the eye around the room. Use peacock for the kitchen area, on cabinets and work surfaces.

Glowing orange is a beacon colour that can be used as a statement in a single lamp, or position an orange neon tube in a dark corner.

Graphite, *glass and neon*

Frosted lavender (**1**) is a great neutral shade: it is soft and unassuming, yet cool and warm, all at once. In open-plan environments such versatile colours are a must to use throughout. Then, create smaller spaces within the room through shapes and colour use.

Architectural colours for open-plan, double-height arenas.

Paint the ceiling in pale sky (**2**) to artificially reduce the height of the room. For fun, you could even paint some clouds as a final touch.

Mid-blue (**3**) can be used for the doors, which could all be made from tinted glass to let in as much light as possible.

Dark teal (**4**) is a strong colour that can be used to draw in an area. Paint a corner or a single wall with this colour and use it as a backdrop for bitter-lime (**5**) accessories. Treat your home like a gallery space, place neon-yellow glass pieces on shelves and spotlight them.

Iridescence *and sparkle*

Use delicate tinted pales for a fairy-tale room.

Be careful with very pale colours like lilac tint (**1**). Always test some paint on the wall first because even the softest shades can seem intense when used all over. Use fairy lights for magical evenings. By day, sunlight will catch on crystals and mirrors, sending sparkles around the room.

1

2

3

Lilac tint (**1**) can be enhanced by mixing it with pearlescent paint, making the walls literally shine.

Use flat, chalky surfaces in here, so the room does not become too kitsch. Sweet candy floss (**2**) can be used for window-sills and skirting-boards.

4

Marshmallow (**3**) is a flatter tone that is perfect for flooring. Go for carpet or painted floor tiles.

5

Cowslip (**5**) is for the furnishings in soft suede or fluffy cashmere blends.

Satin pillows in palest mint (**4**) are beaded with tiny crystals.

Sweet *and sugary*

Take inspiration from your favourite rich desserts with these mouth-watering colours. Paints and surfaces are good enough to eat in creamy, butter-soft leathers, coloured-glass tabletops and shelves as pretty as boiled sweets. Delicate, sugared violet (**1**) is perfect for a pretty bedroom.

Peaches and cream, sugared violets and vanilla mousse.

1

2

3

Vanilla cream (**2**) and honey (**3**) are wonderfully soft and romantic pale shades. Use these tones for the ceiling and the floor. They will also mix perfectly with the main colour in patterns and decoration. Choose faded miniature flower patterns for fabrics and wallpaper, and search out some vintage styles for a truly individual look. Many modern outlets supply whole ranges based on vintage and traditional designs.

4

5

Peach (**4**) and raspberry mousse (**5**) are delicious colours for details and assessories.

Considered *design*

A contemporary fusion of masculine and feminine style.

This room is modern yet sophisticated. Each area and accessory is well thought out and cleverly matched or placed. Dusty mauve (**1**) is an interesting colour since such mid-tones are versatile, working in either a feminine or masculine way.

Dark rabbit-fur grey (**3**) is the main secondary colour. Use it on woodwork and for sueded seats and sofas. This colour works as a shadow shade to the main mauve.

Porcelain blue (**2**) can be used in a dining room for dishes and serving bowls; choose a high-gloss enamelled finish if possible.

Musky rose (**4**) is a wonderfully deep colour, that would be great for heavy curtains and carpets throughout the downstairs areas of the house.

For a touch of glamour, add details in magenta (**5**), such as glass vases and small cashmere cushions.

Heather, amethyst, *mineral blue*

Heather (**1**) is tranquil and relaxing, creating an instantly homely and still environment in any room. For centuries many have believed that purple shades have magical powers that are both stimulating and soothing. Bearing this in mind, a room in this palette should be a haven in which to indulge the senses.

A calming bedroom environment to help you sleep.

Use dark heather (**3**) for the woodwork in the room.

Crystal blue (**2**) is an invigorating colour, so paint the floorboards with it to lift the spirit of the room.

Dark amethyst and mineral blue (**4**, **5**) can be used to paint furniture such as chairs or bedside tables.

This room can change with the seasons. In the warmer months stick to cotton bedcovers in crystal blue and embroidered pillowcases. In the cooler times opt for layers of luxurious quilting on the bed and dyed sheepskin rugs on the floor for extra comfort and warmth.

Sumptuous *indulgence*

Create a haven of luxury with clever colours and textures.

Dusty levels of mauve shades work well with natural colours. Black-cherry mousse (**1**) is a wonderful shade to live with and brings warmth and a touch of glamour to the evenings and a liveliness to the day. Mid-tones are lifted by a clever use of accent shades and tactile surfaces.

Use natural grey (**2**) for the woodwork. In a space with traditional features, pick out the dado rail and ornate fireplace with rich aubergine (**5**).

Champagne (**3**) can be used for the flooring and for heavy, velvet curtains.

Aubergine really gives this room some drama. Use it in mixes for patterned cushions, dark picture frames and graphic shelving.

Light peach (**4**) is a pretty element. Use it for glass wall sconces that send dramatic patterns across the walls. Choose a pink-tinted mirror to hang above the fireplace.

Smooth, *diffused and mellow*

These colours may seem unspecific, but they are utterly beautiful and blend wonderfully from one to the next. Warm lavender (**1**) is the severest of the five shades, but clever use of the natural and greened tones will serve to dampen its intensity.

A sensitive blend of mid-tones creates a pleasing mood.

1

2

3

Neutral shades work very well with lavender since they warm the room and calm the intensity of the floral main colour. Use stone (**2**) for the woodwork and feather armchairs in soft wools or suede for total comfort.

Use straw (**3**) for natural seagrass woven matting.

4

5

Use cooler, greened neutrals (**4**, **5**) for cushions, heavy velvet curtains and misty layers of organdy at the windows. Find large enamelled bowls for the table centre and fill with succulent treats such as figs, cinnamon sweets or lavender-scented cake.

Cyclamen *and vivid pastels*

A pretty blend of colours brightens up a dull room.

Vivid cyclamen (**1**) needs softer tones to subdue its brightness. This palette is perfect for areas that do not get a lot of daylight. Intense shades can liven up windowless areas, such as a stairwell or hallway. Utilize the architectural shapes by painting surfaces in different colours.

If the main shade seems too intense, use pastel violet (**3**) and dusty heather (**2**) on alternate walls. These pretty colours would also be great for the ceiling in the stairwell to reflect maximum light.

Clear, crisp, minty greens (**4**, **5**) are perfect for a painted floor and any woodwork, including the front door and banister.

Feature your home's entrance with refreshing colours and quirky lighting. Why not invest in a modern, green-glass chandelier or light fixture to draw focus?

Graphic *Victorian decoration*

Victorian mauve (**1**) is a gorgeous colour to use with the wallpaper and patterned fabrics that are making a comeback in modern interior design. Many companies produce ranges of wallpaper in contemporary and traditional styles. To ensure a pattern does not overpower the room cover only a single wall.

Introduce wallpaper with patterns and modern prints.

Violet and soft green (**3**) is a classic combination, favoured by the Victorians in particular. This room needs bitter chocolate (**2**) for the woodwork as a graphic edge. Cover this dark shade with your hand on the page and see how instantly 'pretty' the other colours are without its input. Choose a wallpaper with a linear quality that uses these contrasting shades.

The clear greens (**3**, **4**) are perfect for the fabrics in the room.

Mix darker violet (**5**) with the bitter chocolate if the room looks too purple.

Mexican *colonial*

A soft violet-grey enlivened with brick and rich indigo.

Inspired by Mexican painter Frida Kahlo's house, this palette using clay violet (**1**) is typical of a bohemian Mexican colonial dwelling. The rich indigo-blue and earthy red have been copied throughout Mexico and beyond. Kahlo's use of colour in her paintings was dramatic and bold, and this is reflected in her interior design.

Use earth red (**2**) for the flooring. Try a traditional rammed-earth floor, made from compacted earth and sealed with boiled linseed oil, which intensifies the colour and gives a high shine.

Pale blue (**3**) and rich teal (**4**) can be used to paint geometric patterns onto cupboard doors in the kitchen. Find old paintings in charity shops with good use of colour and hang them together on one wall.

Use deep indigo (**5**) for the woodwork and door. Continue this palette outside, since in hot countries living is undertaken both indoors and out.

1930s ocean-liner *glamor*

In this palette, colours are enhanced by the luxurious surfaces. Softest greys, shimmering velvets and deep-pile carpets all make for a decadent interior. Heliotrope (**1**) needs cool, neutral shades to help absorb the brightness of the colour. Bold furniture is inspired by grand ocean liners with sweeping curves.

A decadent palette of elegant colours and cool shapes.

Silver and platinum (**2**, **3**) can be used for glossy details in the room. Paint the doors, window frame and the fireplace with these colours. Highlight details such as door handles, curtain rods and a fireplace with chrome or polished mirrored glass. Cover the top of a low, round table with mirrored glass and accessorize with cocktail glasses and pink champagne.

Striped platinum (**3**) and pink ice (**4**) can be used for the upholstery.

Use pale sea mist (**5**) for the flooring. For a grand approach, lay a pale wood parquet floor.

Windswept *and bracing*

Colours inspired by the beauty of a weathered seashore.

Nothing is more refreshing than a brisk walk along an exposed area of natural coastline. The unusual foliage and plant life in these areas are not seen elsewhere. On stormy days the sky, sea and land merge in waves of purple haze (**1**), creating a harsh and beautiful scene.

1

2

3

4

5

Bring these dramatic colours into the protection of your home for a harmonious palette. The main purple haze (**1**) is the colour of deep storm clouds. Use it on the walls and see how everything else in the room stands out from this rich backdrop.

Sand and pebble (**2**, **3**) are perfect colours for the woodwork. In a bathroom choose natural pebble flooring for a great massage underfoot.

Choose ice blue (**4**) and bleak grey (**5**) for large furniture that will look amazing against the purple. Choose wool for a soft finish.

Ripe, *juicy plum*

Plum (**1**) is decadent and full – a passionate colour not for the fainthearted. Use strong colours like these in a cosy den or a sexy bedroom. Mix these ripened colours with sumptuous surfaces. Choose smooth satin for the bed and soft carpet for the floor. Soft lighting will enhance the deep shades.

Rich, berry tones always produce an extravagant room.

Softer, milkshake pinks (**2**, **3**) can be used for the woodwork and the furniture, such as a chest of drawers, armoire or sideboard. Use lots of mirrors to bring in maximum light.

Highlights of forest fruits, like blackberry (**4**) and blueberry (**5**), really give depth to this luscious environment. Do not be afraid of such dark colours: use them with confidence and the end result will always be successful. Cover old armchairs in deepest-berry velvets for total indulgence. These mouthwatering tones will enhance the plum tone of the walls without being overpowering.

Art deco *outlining*

A graphic black outline underscores these stylized pinks.

Look to the art deco period of the 1930s, an era in design characterized by geometric shapes, clean lines and simple use of colour, for a dramatic finish. Blackcurrant (**1**) is lifted with cool pinks and a silvery green. Create a dramatic entrance to your home using these colours.

Cool pink (**3**) can be used in recesses or alcoves to flood light into that area. Use black (**2**) to outline shapes in the room. Woodwork, banisters and crown moulding can all be black. For a truly decadent look, go for a glossy black floor; it will reflect the colour in the room.

Hot pink (**4**) is for some giant ostrich feathers to stand in a glossy, black vase in the corner of the room.

Use silver grey (**5**) for the furniture. Paint pieces this colour and outline cupboard doors and drawer handles in black.

Bohemian *aubergine*

This is a wonderful palette of rich, sexy darks and vibrant, modern brights. Aubergine (**1**) has become a very popular interior shade. Many contemporary bars and restaurants use a similar tone to create an instantly warm and cosy environment.

Eccentric, rich colours for a truly original setting.

Deep aubergine (**1**) makes a fabulous wallcovering, intense and sultry. Use a varnish or gloss over the colour to intensify the richness.

Chocolate (**3**) is for the dark, exotic furniture in the room. An intricate, carved wooden door from the Far East can be topped with glass and made into a table.

Lavender, orange bloom and bright tangerine (**2**, **4**, **5**) can be used to create unusual dinner settings with hand-painted dishes and coloured glassware.

All colours can be mixed together in intricate Persian rugs to cover the floor and some of the walls.

Neutrals

Timeless *quality*

A traditional palette with a twist.

A dark, greyed neutral can be a cosy colour. Mix bark (**1**) with softened dusky pinks, old-fashioned red and soft sand for instantly comfortable surroundings. This palette offers soothing background tones and modern accents, making it an easy colour scheme to get right.

1

2

3

Choose comfortable soft furnishings for a room that you can truly relax in. The mix of dark and light colours makes it an equally great place to be in the daytime or in the evening with soft candlelight.

4

Use soft pinks (**2**, **3**) for patterned rugs on the floors. The darker shade is for heavy, woven curtains.

5

Faded red (**4**) can be used to cover small pieces of furniture, such as a footstool or nested tables.

Sand (**5**) is a lovely, rich yellowed neutral, great for tiling around a fireplace.

Room *to contemplate*

Soft mink (**1**) is cocooning and protective. Wrap yourself in these warming, autumn shades for a quiet place to read and think, away from the hustle and bustle of the city. Houses today can be busy and noisy, so it is very important to find an area within the home that is peaceful and private where you can relax.

Soft yet invigorating colours for a quiet reading area.

Invest in a designer chair and have it covered in a graphic, 1950s-style fabric to make a centrepiece. Although the colours are flat, you can experiment with the details in this room. Remember, this is your own private space so do whatever you want.

Keep large pieces of furniture pale and simple for a restful atmosphere. Use warm white (**2**) for the floor and the ceiling. Keep the window bare to let in the maximum amount of light.

Rusted oranges (**4**, **5**) can be used for a fun retro reading lamp and a cosy checked blanket.

Rose-tinted *romantic*

A discreet, sentimental palette of natural shades.

Natural string (**1**) is an uncomplicated, easy background colour. You can create almost any design with this tone as a base. Such colours are reminiscent of a simpler way of life, not driven by the industrial age. Coordinate this palette with natural surfaces and fabrics.

In a bathroom use natural stone with a sandy quality for the bath and sink. The same stone can be used to cover the floor. Alternatively, opt for dark wood floorboards.

Dusky rose (**3**) and madder red (**4**) can be created from natural dyes. Bring some much-needed colour into this room with bowls of dried rose petals.

Use unbleached linen (**5**) and organic cotton for towels and curtains. There are no man-made materials in this room. Ointments and cosmetics are made from organic ingredients and stored in glass jars with hand-written labels.

Oyster *shell*

Use rich oyster (**1**) in a bedroom or bathroom for a soft, relaxing mood. You could mix this colour with an iridescent or sparkle medium to create a stunning, subtle shimmer on the walls. By day this would light up the room and by night, flickering candles will illuminate the sparkles.

This low-level palette features exaggerated natural tones.

1

2

3

The accent tones in this palette are intensified, pearlescent colours. Cool and pretty, these shades would work well mixed in patterns or as flat, solid expanses.

In a bedroom use soft grey-blue (**3**) for the woodwork and paint the bedside tables to match.

4

Use delicate mint (**2**) for glassware and lighting. In the bathroom fit a glass shower cubicle in this colour.

5

Use heather (**4**) and pink (**5**) for the bedcovers. Choose a delicately beaded or embroidered throw for an embellished touch.

Jungle *camouflage*

Create a fun indoor play area for children.

Bring the outdoors in with an extreme playroom for all the kids using sand (**1**). Use ropes and camouflage netting to section off areas of the room and put rubber tiles on the floor for protection. Fit climbing rings to the walls and hang hammocks up instead of using chairs.

1

2

3

Think of army training camps and outward-bound schools to create an indoor den that will keep the children happy for years.

Use natural sand colours (**1**, **2**) for the walls. Paint the darker colour halfway up and the lighter colour to the ceiling.

Use khaki (**3**) for the flooring, either rubber or scuff-proof linoleum.

4

5

Rich browns (**4**, **5**) can be used for the fun elements in the room. Paint the children's names graffiti-style across the wall and have a wipe-clean area for finger painting.

For the truly daring, why not put a sandpit in the middle of the floor?

Straw, *wheat and corn*

A palette inspired by countryside colours can work equally well in a city dwelling. If you want to bring a touch of the real and the rustic to a modern flat, then look no further than this straw (**1**) shade. Reminiscent of sun-scorched afternoons on country roads, these tones will give a boost to any tired area.

Ripening fields inspire yellowed neutrals.

This colour palette could easily be utilized throughout the ground floor of a home or within an open-plan environment. Soft, cream walls can easily move from the kitchen to the living area to the dining room.

Use red earth (**2**) tiles for the flooring. In an area where you want more warmth, such as the living room, place a large, patterned rug in natural ochre (**3**) shades by the hearth.

Summer green (**4**) can be used for cupboard doors and upholstery.

Use pretty touches of peach (**5**) in watercolour pictures and ceramics.

Discreet, *considerate, reserved*

The most colourless of palettes can often be the most striking.

It sometimes takes more courage to leave things out of a design than to put things in. Milk (**1**) needs simple themes and uncluttered rooms to make for a very rewarding interior design. If you can live simply and hide your clutter, then this clean, elegant colour is for you.

1

2

3

Mix and match these harmonious shades of pale in any form you like. If you want a darker emphasis in the room then simply make the hessian (**5**) highlight colour your major secondary colour, perhaps in the form of scrubbed wooden surfaces.

Natural materials would work best in here, such as a limestone floor that emulates all the tones in the palette.

4

5

Stack creamy ceramic plates on open wooden shelves. Remove all food from its packaging and put into tin or glass containers for a uniform finish.

Buttermilk *and olive*

Buttermilk (**1**) is a gently warmed neutral. This type of colour will create a soft yet sophisticated background. Choose natural linen and woven fabrics for this room, and opt for naturally dyed surfaces if at all possible. You could even try covering parts of the walls in fabric; panels give the best result.

Mix warm neutrals and olive green for elegant dining.

Green is said to behave just like a neutral. Stone and flat green (**2**, **3**) can be used as the background shades, perhaps on the flooring and woodwork in the room. You could keep the mix simple, or use these colours in a pattern of psychedelic swirls for retro accessories, such as storage boxes, cushions or seat covers.

Use rich olive (**4**) and lime (**5**) in shocking glassware, or collect vintage, patterned Bakelite cups and saucers to display.

Tropical, *exotic palm house*

A palette inspired by the palm greenhouses of the 1920s.

A whitened, ivory (**1**) -coloured, sun-filled room filled with exotic plants, such as palms, orchids and ferns, creates an indoor garden in a sunny living room or kitchen. Take reference from traditional palm houses with ornate windows, French doors and large, plant-filled pots.

Use pebble (**2**) for the tiled flooring. For a high-tech twist, invest in underfloor heating to keep a tropical temperature all year round.

Use levels of green for a calming, tranquil atmosphere. Softened fern (**3**) is a great colour for the woodwork and for the plant pots in the room.

Mix green leaf (**4**) and orchid (**5**) with white in exotic floral prints for cushions and curtains or blinds. Match paint to real flower colours for a special twist.

Choose wicker furniture and glass tabletops.

Latte, *espresso and cappuccino*

This decadent palette of caffé latte (**1**) browns and neutrals could easily be inspired by an expensive restaurant or coffee-shop interior. These simple tones work well together to create a neutral yet luxurious background. This colour mix would work well in the kitchen, living room or dining area.

A frothy mix of creams and aromatic coffee colour.

A simple, classic mix of colours for creating a stylish atmosphere.

Use café au lait (**2**), a subtle shade darker than the main colour, for the woodwork.

Use coffee bean (**4**) for an area of the room, such as a chimney breast, or pick out features such as beams or alcoves. Offset this dramatic dark colour with framed black-and-white photography on the pale wall in the room.

Use cream (**5**) for fluffy sheepskin cushions and a cashmere throw on the brown leather (**3**) sofa.

Golden, *filtered sunlight*

A sun-filled palette brings cheer and warmth to the home.

Use levels of golden yellow and papyrus (**1**) to mimic the effect of the sun being filtered through the shades into the room. These tones are great neutral colours for a guest room that may not get used as often as other rooms, or use them in a kitchen, bathroom or bedroom. Such a palette has wide appeal.

1

2

3

Lemon mousse (**2**) can be used for the bed linens. Stripe it with lemon butter (**3**) for the duvet cover and chair covers.

Use bright gold (**4**) for hand-painted details around the door and windows. There are many stencil companies that offer quick and easy patterns and flowers to adorn the walls.

4

5

Hen's egg (**5**) can be used to paint wooden furniture, such as an old-fashioned school chair and a simple table with a drawer.

Place a vase of daisies on the table whenever there are guests using the room.

African *adobe*

This palette takes its references from traditional African dwellings, clay (**1**), adobe houses and naturally dyed yarns used to weave indigenous fabrics. If you find a piece of fabric at home or abroad that you simply love, why not create a whole room around that one item?

Earthy hues that can be cleverly mixed for the modern home.

If you can source it, use natural distemper or limewash on the walls for a flat, simple finish. Adobe, or dried earth, is used in one-third of the housing in the world today. This ancient but beautiful finish is being revived by modern architects.

Use African carved wood for the furniture. In large towns you can find an importer of exotic furniture or check online – just beware of shoddy imitations.

Rich Persian red (**5**) and adobe (**4**) can be mixed with the main colour in traditional woven fabrics to drape over furniture and walls.

Bold *colour blocking*

Soft beige is enlivened with jewel-coloured accents.

This is a classic 1960s palette of biscuit (**1**) shades, intense greens and turquoises. You can still find objects such as mugs, teapots and storage tins in the original, swirling, psychedelic patterns. Use these sparingly and focus on using clever blocks of colour.

1

2

3

This palette could easily work in an open-plan environment, since the soft colours (**1**, **2**, **3**) can be used to split areas of the room to denote kitchen, living room and bedroom while the stronger colours (**4**, **5**) can be used to segregate with bold painted stripes.

4

5

Keep all the floors pale in willow (**3**) for a light effect.

Use the stronger colours such as cactus (**4**) and teal (**5**), to create blocks of colour on the walls and around the room with one-off pieces of furniture and coloured window blinds that stand out against the paler colours.

Stone, *rose quartz and amethyst*

Stone (**1**) sounds like a cold colour, but there are many types of stone that can be used in the home. Choose a yellow- or red-based stone, such as limestone, for a warm feeling. This natural material can be used throughout a bathroom or kitchen for the floor, the surfaces and the tiling.

A palette of natural mineral tones can be pretty and feminine.

Pale stones are nearly always mixed with light or neutral colours. Mix with pretty levels of rose quartz and amethyst for a stronger use of colour.

Rose quartz (**3**) can be used for all of the remaining walls.

Use pretty tones of amethyst (**4**, **5**) for towels, soaps and chair covers.

Accessorize the bathroom with natural lumps of crystal and amethyst, which will look stunning against the stone. Direct lighting towards them, or light with candles for maximum effect.

A garden room *with lavender*

Fill a room that opens to the outdoors with floral shades.

This palette is perfect in a room that opens out onto a garden. If one entire wall opens out into the garden then the definition between inside and out can be pleasantly blurred. Since the area should be filled with plants, this palette uses muted oatmeal (**1**) as a very subtle backdrop.

Use natural stone paving slabs on the floor, and run a water channel around the edge of the room to irrigate the plants.

Use muted oatmeal (**1**) for walls, or mix it with white and pale lavender (**3**) for a striped, hand-painted finish. Alternatively, mix these colours in checked or polka-dot fabrics to cover the chairs.

Use garden lilac and purple (**4**, **5**) for plant pots. Mix with galvanized steel if you want a rather more industrial feel.

Business-like *and smart*

As many more of us are working from home, we need areas within the house suitable for meeting clients or holding meetings. Home-office environments do not need to be as formal as the real thing, but you can create an air of professionalism with smart olive (**1**) colours.

Shades of tailored neutrals create a chic working area.

Take references from a good tailor: use only the best-quality materials and make sure everything in this room fits properly. With clever storage and classy furniture, the office can quickly be packed away to create a stylish dining area.

Soft green (**2**) and faded charcoal (**3**) should be used for glass worktops and carpeting for a relaxing, tranquil atmosphere.

For a slick finish, choose pinstriped fabrics or tweeds in deep grey (**4**) for the chair covers.

Dark navy (**5**) can be used for seamless cupboard doors, that open with just a touch.

Embellished, *Indian exotic*

A richly decorated room based on India's palaces.

Once upon a time, the Taj Mahal was decorated with real jewels. Rubies and emeralds that sparkled in the sunshine were carefully embedded into the walls of the palace. Build a highly decorated room reminiscent of the elaborate palaces of India by using a base colour of dust (**1**).

Use darkest emerald (**5**) for the woodwork and a heavily framed mirror.

Use beaded sari fabrics for curtains and cushion covers. Every surface in this room can be covered in some kind of rich ornamentation.

Faded red and deep ruby (**3**, **4**) can be used for patterned upholstery. Choose traditional paisleys.

Hang coloured glass lanterns from the ceiling to cast pretty patterns around the room.

Deep khaki, *cobalt and black*

Deep khaki (**1**) needs bright, uplifting colours to stop it from appearing drab. Violet-blue (**3**) and cobalt (**4**) are great, strong pigment colours that really shine when used in any environment. Use geometric patterning, either in an area of wallpaper behind the dining table or even as a feature atop the table itself.

A graphic palette of dark and light shades.

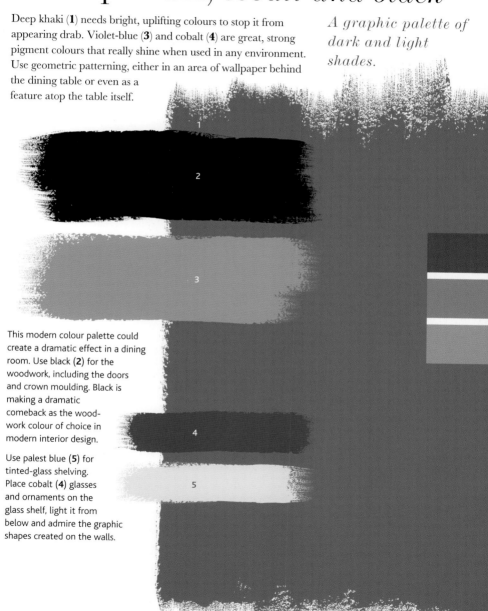

This modern colour palette could create a dramatic effect in a dining room. Use black (**2**) for the woodwork, including the doors and crown moulding. Black is making a dramatic comeback as the wood-work colour of choice in modern interior design.

Use palest blue (**5**) for tinted-glass shelving. Place cobalt (**4**) glasses and ornaments on the glass shelf, light it from below and admire the graphic shapes created on the walls.

Greys

Cool, *clean and contemporary*

A great, modern palette for a stylish kitchen environment.

Granite (**1**) is dark enough to offer warmth. Combine it with cool greys and blues to create an instantly stylish area, perhaps a totally high-tech kitchen. Choose stainless steel appliances and spend a little extra on the details, such as designer taps, light switches and door handles.

1

2

3

Ice (**2**) and aluminium (**3**) are perfect for contemporary kitchen units. Choose ice-tinted glass for the work surfaces for a clean style. Lighting is very important in the kitchen – always have good, directional lighting, such as spotlights, around the work surfaces.

4

5

Check out some of the modern, resin floor tiles currently available. Glass-effect floor tiles can give a room a light and modern feeling instantly.

Slate blue and deep ocean (**4**, **5**) can be used for blinds, seat covers and serving bowls to add splashes of colour to the room.

Sunshine *bright*

Concrete (**1**) and yellow are a good combination. With cool levels, warm shades and darker tones, you can play with shadow and light here. In a kitchen, think carefully about where the sun comes in in the morning so your breakfast area is assured a sunny wake-up.

Flat grey enlivened with a burst of sunshine yellow.

Yellow is a common colour to use in the kitchen. By combining it with grey shades, you can create a modern design rather than the usual country-kitchen look.

Choose pale ash (**2**) for the cupboard doors and chrome for handles and appliances.

Rich cream and lemon (**3**, **4**) can be used for plates, cups and serving bowls. Go for a lemon worktop for a refreshing change.

Sunshine (**5**) is a strong colour and should be used sparingly. Paint the back-door panels and cover the chair seats with it, striped with grey if you prefer.

Warm *and harmonious*

Bright turquoise livens up a medley of neutral shades.

Neutral tones always look good layered on top of each other. Natural sand and stone colours can be used in almost any combination for a soft, cosy, comfortable environment. Here, pebble (**1**) is enhanced with warming natural shades. The contrasting turquoise gives a modern kick.

1

2

3

Grey walls are becoming very chic. Many of us associate grey with drab and cold exteriors of buildings, but we can see here that warmer tones of grey are incredibly effective.

Use blond and pale wood (**2**, **3**) for the flooring and the window and door frames since they will lift the grey.

4

5

Chocolate and turquoise (**4**, **5**) are a classic design combination. Use brown leather for furniture and picture frames. Accessorize with a turquoise cashmere blanket and a turquoise telephone. Stand a large rock of real turquoise on the mantle.

Lichen, *sage and willow*

Tinted neutrals form a highly sophisticated level of colours. The soft tones of lichen (**1**) coloured with green or pink create a subtle glow, and change dramatically depending on whether the light is natural or artificial. Neutrals are the perfect blank canvas upon which to paint the picture of your interior design.

Green-tinted grey makes a natural backdrop.

Sage (**3**) is a stunning level of green to live with. It is natural, pretty and relaxing all at once. You could use sage to paint floorboards or kitchen or bathroom cabinets, or use it for a luxurious carpet in a bedroom or living room.

Willow (**2**) is a fairly bright green and can be used on floor-length curtains or for any woodwork .

Lime white (**4**) brings light to this room. Paint the ceiling and the floor with it for maximum reflection in the room.

Rose (**5**) brings a touch of prettiness. Fill a vase with pink blooms such as peonies.

Precious *metal*

An indulgent palette of pales for a salon-style interior.

This palette is rather impractical for many homes. Soft, tinted layers of whites and silver grey (**1**) would not last long in a family environment. However, if you are looking for a style statement, there can be little more classy than this sophisticated level of precious metals.

1

2

3

Pale bone (**2**) is a wonderfully soft tone for a deep-pile carpet or rug. Reflection and glass are very important in this room. Use mirrors in a clever way: collect antique bevelled-edge mirrors and cover a single wall with them to bring maximum light into a dark room.

4

5

Use darker grey (**3**) for the woodwork and furnishings as a graphic edge. Find 1930s-style curved chairs, and maybe a chaise longue, and cover them with shimmering silk velvet.

Light ceramic (**4**) and dusk (**5**) can be used for layers of diaphanous curtains at the windows.

Weathered *and seashore fresh*

Lead white (**1**) is reminiscent of the colours of wooden houses by the seashore. The salt air and harsh, coastal breezes break down paint and give surfaces a wonderful, natural matt, sandblasted finish. Coastal living has its own design ethos, which can be recreated in any building, even in the city.

A palette of sea-foam colours, scrubbed and washed by sea air.

Lead white (**1**) is perfectly complemented by a medley of sea greens and weatherboard blues. Choose wooden surfaces where possible. Flat paint is best: it can be watered down and used as a thin, light wash on wood to achieve an instantly weathered look.

Use sea foam (**2**) to paint wooden floorboards or for a simple linoleum flooring. Sky (**3**) is a great neutral colour to choose for bathroom fixtures or for kitchen cupboards.

Sea heather (**4**) and thistle (**5**) can be used for solid, handmade earthenware plates and bowls.

Glowing *accents*

With accents, you can easily change your interior colour.

For a totally versatile interior choose ash (**1**) for the walls and simply build your design onto this blank page. By choosing brighter colours for the accents and highlights, it is easy and economical to change the look of the room when you feel like something new.

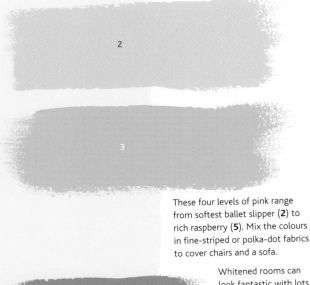

These four levels of pink range from softest ballet slipper (**2**) to rich raspberry (**5**). Mix the colours in fine-striped or polka-dot fabrics to cover chairs and a sofa.

Whitened rooms can look fantastic with lots of colourful accessories. Paint shelves and tables in geranium (**4**), or light surfaces from beneath with pink strip lights.

Position coloured fairy lights in any of the pink shades in dark corners of the room. These wonderful pink tones will positively glow against the whitened walls.

Subtle *tints*

Tinted whites have always been popular interior colours. It is quite amazing what a difference such a subtle tint of colour can make. Choose creamy vanilla (**1**). The accent colours of honey and cinnamon will be reflected in the white paint, perfectly complementing the creamy tint.

A perfect palette for a welcoming kitchen nook.

Linen (**2**) is a great shade, not too bright, but balmy and sunny enough to bring some cheer into any room. Use it for upholstery and curtains.

String (**3**) is a neutral shade but has a warming, pink undertone to keep the room cosy. Use it on the work surfaces and kitchen cupboards.

Cinnamon (**4**) is a great kitchen colour. Use it in a rustic style with terracotta tiles on the floor, and Mediterranean-style handmade bowls and plates. For something more modern, mix it with a metallic decorative finish for copper detail on the woodwork.

Powdered *cosmetics*

Take inspiration from cosmetics for a girly bedroom.

Marble (**1**) is the delicate foundation colour for this room. Build the look on top of it with fragile layers of rouge and shimmering eye-shadow pinks. To complete the look, accessorize with lipstick shades of deep plum on shiny glass vases and polished tabletops.

These pinked levels are flattering and sensitive. In a bedroom, choose shades that are delicate or softened with white for a more subtle approach.

Choose simple shapes of furniture. Mix the eye-shadow pinks (**2**, **3**) with a very subtle pearlescent decorative finish to cover the bedside tables, drawers and armoire.

Dusty lilac (**4**) can be used for the flooring and bed linens.

Finish off the room with accents of plum (**5**). Use it for super-glossy woodwork, and paint the bed frame for a glamorous touch.

Playful *naivety*

This is a room of contrasts: silver fox (**1**) is brought to life with bright sunny pigments. This palette is suited to a room with maximum natural light that will enhance the freshness of the bright colours. Choose shiny, modern surfaces, such as moulded plastic seating.

Mix cheerful tones of blue and yellow with a tranquil grey.

1

2

3

Silver fox (**1**) makes for a flat, blanketed foundation. Cover all of the walls and the floor with this colour and simply use the remaining colours to pick out details in the room.

Use frozen blue (**2**) on the ceiling for a lightened, airy feeling.

4

Summer sky (**3**) can be used for the woodwork. The naive use of primary colours will give this room a childlike, almost dollhouse, quality.

5

In a bathroom, mix and match the accessories in blue and yellow (**4**, **5**) for a playful theme.

Dusk, *half light, sundown*

Delicate sunset shades reflect light around a room.

As the sun is setting, a strange half-light occurs no matter where you are. It casts unusual shadows and reflects strange colours around an interior. It is an exceptionally beautiful moment in time. With dusk (**1**) and these shades of sunset pink, we try to capture that moment.

1

2

3

Use these colours in a room that catches the evening light. In summer, this light will naturally heat up the room and give a glow to everything within.

Dusk (**1**), a pretty, soft grey, is warmed with tints of sunset pink (**3**, **4**) and bold, burning orange (**5**).

4

Use dove grey (**2**) for a feather-filled sofa in velvet or suede. Cover the sofa with scatter cushions in all shades of pink and orange.

5

On the grey walls hang orange-tinted glass lamps that reflect around the room and continue to warm the environment long after sunset.

Turning *leaves*

In nature, as winter approaches the light becomes less bright and the trees change colour from green to russets and browns. Rich colours like cashmere (**1**) have inspired painters for centuries. Take note of the seasons and be inspired by the new colours that each has to offer.

Flattened autumn shades can be rich and inviting.

These colours could make a wonderful kitchen or dining area. With cashmere on the walls, paint the cupboards and cabinets a richer level of mocha (**2**).

Choose russet (**3**) for the work surfaces and tiling.

Go for a dark, stained wood floor for a more cosy atmosphere. Bitter chocolate (**5**) is a rich and warming colour. If you have an open fire, source a dramatic mantle and stain it in this dark colour.

Peach (**4**) can be mixed with russet and chocolate in checked fabrics for seat covers and curtains.

Fake *furs*

A design inspired by fake-fur throws is utterly indulgent.

Today, fake fur is so good that we have no need for the real thing. Throws, bedcovers and rugs in rabbit fur (**1**) and dyed sheepskin have become an integral part of interior design.

Why not layer fur around the room, like in the bedroom of a Russian princess?

1

2

3

Even fake fur has a wonderful, shimmering, soft quality to it, with several shades and colours apparent in every piece. Use subtle levels of mink and grey (**2**) in a bedroom to emulate the colours in the fur bed throw.

4

Use dusty heather (**3**) for the woodwork and a painted floor for a pretty, but still cool, edge.

5

Dye some sheepskins in deep purple (**5**) and have them on the floor around the bed.

Use feathers dyed mauve (**4**) to trim the lampshade and the edge of cushions to continue the textural theme.

Winter grey *and iced mint*

Fresh, cool mint and dove (**1**) make a wonderful partnership.
This colour scheme works well in a bathroom or a modern,
streamlined kitchen. Choose easy-to-clean, waterproof surfaces,
such as tiles and paint with an antifungal treatment to prevent
mildew; the crisp colours will
stay fresher for longer.

*A refreshing palette
of icy mints and
cool greys.*

With the main warmed mid-grey
on the walls, the delicate shades of
green and mint will be able to take
over the room.

Use smoky ice (**2**) for the
woodwork and flooring.
Opt for something with
a flawless finish such as
linoleum or bonded
rubber tiles.

The three shades of
mint (**3**, **4**, **5**) can be
used in varying degrees.
Use the palest shade for the larger
furniture, such as the bathroom
fixtures or cupboard doors in the
kitchen. Use green-tinted glass for
the shower doors and counters.

Timeless *desert detailing*

Classic layers of greys and natural, sandblasted shades.

Natural shades used in interiors often evoke an uncomplicated, unchallenging atmosphere. The colours in this palette are synonymous with a simpler way of life. Even in a city flat, mineral grey (**1**) can create an unpretentious environment.

Nothing in this room is flashy or ostentatious. Simple pleasures of cooking, eating and spending time with friends and family are the backbone of this room.

The oven and a large wooden table are the focus. Colourwash the scrubbed wooden surfaces with pebble (**3**) for a lighter finish.

Choose natural slate for the floor, but invest in underfloor heating to warm up the room.

Warm terracotta colours (**4**, **5**) can be used for rustic earthenware serving bowls and tactile, handmade mugs.

A neon *lift*

There is an infinite variety of grey shades. You can easily tint basic greys with warmer or cooler shades to complement the other colours in your palette. A flagstone grey (**1**) is the perfect backdrop colour. The soft, dusty shades are lifted with a clever use of neon brights.

Grey makes the perfect backdrop to bold, garish brights.

Muted grey (**2**) can be used for the woodwork. Create artificial panels on the walls with wooden beading and fill them with this plaster colour for a traditional, panelled-room look.

Within these panels you can frame pieces of furniture or accessories. Cover a single chair with neon pink (**4**) velvet and place it against the grey backdrop on one side of the room. On the opposite side, place the same chair covered in grey fabric against a plaster backdrop and accessorize with a neon yellow (**5**) cushion. Place alternate pink and yellow single vases along the mantle.

Titanium *and stainless steel*

Choose architectural finishes for a cool, modern kitchen.

Take inspiration from the American architect Frank Gehry and his design for the Guggenheim Museum in Bilbao, Spain. Vast, curving expanses of polished metal panels look dramatic and give a clean, hi-tech finish. Choose steel (**1**) for walls and metal sheeting for cabinets.

Utilize the natural quality of stainless-steel surfaces with their dulled, polished finish. This reflects colour, but is not too shiny or overpowering.

Pale silver (**2**) can be used for high-gloss flooring. Use either polished concrete or glass-effect resin tiles.

Use cool blue (**3**) tones to complement the amount of grey in the room, and choose bright-blue (**4**) tinted glass for the work surfaces.

Dark navy (**5**) can be used for seat covers. For a classy finish, why not choose navy pinstriped suiting fabrics or a smooth wool flannel?

Index

Charcoal *and russet*

This charcoal (**1**) is warmed up with the use of natural browns and rich autumn shades. Use the deep colour to create an intimate, lavish interior. Darker shades offer an instant feeling of quality and grounding in a room. Use white on the ceiling to prevent the space from becoming sombre.

Dark grey tones can be luxurious in a simple dining area.

For total decadence, use a piece of polished marble as the tabletop in soft, warm grey colours (**2**). Such a centrepiece would need little decoration, but the weight of it may require extra support in the floor.

Warmed chestnut (**3**) can be used for leather seating around the table.

Use rust (**4**) for the curtains and the light fixtures for an autumnal glow.

Deep berry (**5**) can be used for an opulent dinner service. Fill bowls with deep-berry red roses for the centre of the table.

How to use *this book*

(1) Colour-coded bullets

These correspond to the colour chapter that you are in.

(2) Overview

An overview of the colour scheme and the mood it evokes.

(3) Inspirations

The inspiration behind the colour choices. This section tells you about the main colour for the room.

(4) Explanatory text

How to apply the featured colour scheme to a real-life interior.

(5) Main colour

Take this book to your local DIY shop and ask them to match a test pot to this colour. Paint a square of colour on your chosen wall and let it dry, paint always changes colour when it dries. Live with the colour for a day or two to see if you really do love it before committing to a whole room.

(6) Tonal varieties of the main colour

If you are not entirely happy with the main colour, try one of these great alternatives.

(7) Accent colours

These can be used for an adjacent wall, for woodwork or to match to upholstery fabrics. The colours may be darker or lighter tones of the main shade, neutral shades to balance a room or complementary colours to contrast.

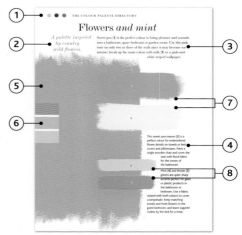

(8) Highlight colours

These can take the form of a sharp injection of colour against a pale wall, such as a red glass vase in a pale blue interior or the final balancing tone in a range of harmonious colours, such as deep chocolate brown in a room of luxurious coffee tones. The highlight colours, although only used in small quantities, are often the most important shades of all because they complete the design.

How to use this *book*

Use this handy pull-out key as a quick reference
to how each of the palettes function.

Credits

Quarto would like to thank and acknowledge the following for supplying photographs reproduced in this book:

2 David George www.david-george.co.uk
9 Sukey Parnell
11 Eric Roth / Susan Sargent Design
www.ericrothphoto.com www.susansargent.com
12 Botanica / Getty Images
16 Sukey Parnell
18 Tim Imrie / Abode
20 Stephen J.Whitehorne / Myriad Images
21 Jan Baldwin / Narratives
22 Bonga Design – contemporary lighting for the domestic & commercial market
www.bongadesignlighting.co.uk
23 Gareth Brown / Corbis

24 David George www.david-george.co.uk
28, 29, 30, 31 Sukey Parnell
36, 60, 80, 106 Jan Baldwin / Narratives
132, 158, 188 David George
www.david-george.co.uk
214 Jan Baldwin / Narratives
234 Lindsey Stock / Myriad Images

All other illustrations and photographs are the copyright of Quarto Publishing plc. While every effort has been made to credit contributors, Quarto would like to apologise should there have been any omissions or errors, and would be pleased to make the appropriate correction for future editions of the book.

Acknowledgments

I must thank a few people, without whom, this book would never have become anything more than a never-ending mountain of colour references and painted swatches.

Firstly, thank you to the lovely folk at Quarto for having the faith in me to put this thing together, for putting up with my perfectionist tendencies and for allowing me to learn from them, especially Kate, Moira and Penny. Thank you to Anna and Claudia for their patience in picture research and to Stephen for sorting out problems in a very gentlemanly fashion. A very special thank you to Trisha Telep for her boundless enthusiasm and energy, and for her illicit midnight copy drops! Thanks to Sukey Parnell for her willingness to shoot some extra (gorgeous) pictures, and for her continued good advice and creative support. I would like to dedicate this book to Iain, who has taught me to see the beauty in every day; and who has even offered to marry me, in the middle of all this madness!

I think that writing a book on colour is always intimidating – there are far too many beautiful colours and combinations in the world to fit in to any book. I hope that this book will help others to appreciate our fascinating planet and to understand the joy of finding beauty in our simple everyday experiences.

Colour accuracy

Unfortunately for anyone who uses colour, it is always limiting when trying to reproduce real colour in a printed book, due to the limited colours in printing inks. However, great length and pain has gone into achieving good colour representation in this book, which can be reproduced in your home, by you. The positive outcome of this is that your final interior will definitely be much more exciting than the flat colour on these pages!

It is important to remember that in printing there may be very slight alterations in the final colour. Also, paint colour may vary slightly from one batch to another, so always try to buy colour made in the same batch.